NEVADA CENTRAL

Sagebrush

NARROW GAUGE

Something is lost beyond the mountains
... Go and find it.

MALLORY HOPE FERRELL

Sagebrush
NARROW GAUGE

Once upon a time in the American West there ran a most improbable railway. Seeking the bonanza of gold and silver lodes, it ran down through the years with an eclectic collection of equipment over a high desert and canyon right-of-way, devoid of any population, unless you count an occasional miner, cowboy or longhorn steer.

OTHER RAILROAD BOOKS BY MALLORY HOPE FERRELL

Heimburger House Publishing Company
7236 West Madison Street
Forest Park, Illinois, 60130 USA
www.heimburgerhouse.com

Library of Congress Control No. 2010924142
ISBN No. 978-0-911581-61-4
Layout and Design: Mallory Hope Ferrell, Rachel L. Boger
Dustjacket and frontispiece artwork, John Coker, collection of Paul Harr
Rear dustjacket illustration by John Signor

First edition.
Printed in Hong Kong.

DEDICATION

WARD WALRATH KIMBALL
1914-2002

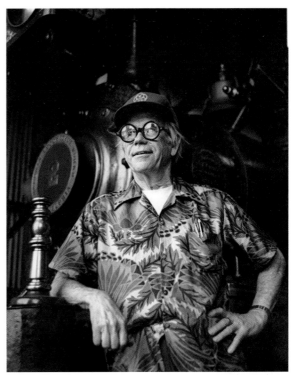

TO WARD KIMBALL, an American legend. One of Walt Disney's original animators, winner of two Academy Award Oscars, Ward also led the famed Dixieland jazz group "Firehouse Five Plus Two."

In 1938, Ward saved Nevada Central's 2-6-0 *Sidney Dillon* and with Betty, his wife for 66 years, built the Grizzly Flats Railroad in their backyard. Ward also collected tin-plate toy trains and antique fire engines, housing them in buildings near the Grizzly Flats enginehouse.

Walt Disney said he was "the only man I would call a genius." He was the ultimate railfan. I was happy to call this multi-talented man my friend.

-Mallory Hope Ferrell

Ward Kimball's story board drawing for Disney's "Dumbo" (1938).

ACKNOWLEDGEMENTS

AFTER MORE THAN A HALF-CENTURY OF RE-SEARCH and collecting, I am indebted to a great number of individuals and institutions. While many sources are named in the captions, and on the Contributors page, special mention is in order for a number of people. Austin resident Wally Trapnell has prodded me and offered assistance for many years. He was especially helpful in locating historic photographs and information. Wally, who owns the Stokes Castle, also helped me retrace the Austin City Railway grades on Lander Hill and commissioned John Signor's dustjacket painting.

For more than 30 years Kyle K. Wyatt, now curator of history at the California State Railroad Museum, has "fed" me old newspaper articles, photographs, research and roster information. Kyle was interested in the project, and his suggestions pointed me in the right direction and to other sources.

Garrie L. Tufford was another great source of accurate material. He was able to determine the identity and origin of the first two Nevada Central (NC) locomotives that had previously been misidentified. Garrie was also helpful in searching out illustrations and restoring faded images.

Mapwork, an essential element in any historical work, was again accomplished in style by Larry Larsen. Likewise, the scale drawings by Robert D. Bailey add another dimension to the book. Artist Jim Scancarelli added his talents by taking time out from his day job of drawing the famed comic strip Gasoline Alley. The drawing of maps, plans and sketches all required an inordinate amount of research, and my thanks go out to Larry, Bob and Jim.

Additional research and photographic help came from Greg Maxwell, who researched the NC's motor cars; Cornelius W. Hauck, who provided photos and data; local historian Jerry R. Mock and Robert W. Brown, editor of the Narrow Gauge & Short Line Gazette.

Historical institutions that opened their files for me included the Nevada Historical Society, North Central Nevada Historical Society, Churchill County Museum, California State Railroad Museum, Nevada State Railroad Museum, North East Nevada Museum, DeGolyer Library of Southern Methodist University and the University of Nevada-Reno Library.

Researching and writing about a subject as remote and obscure as the Nevada Central and its associated feeder lines was no easy task. However, it was made interesting and enjoyable by the many people I encountered "on the trail." My thanks to each of you.

-Mallory Hope Ferrell

MIXED TRAIN SCHEDULE
(TABLE OF CONTENTS)

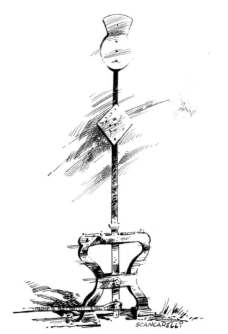

Drawing by Jim Scancarelli

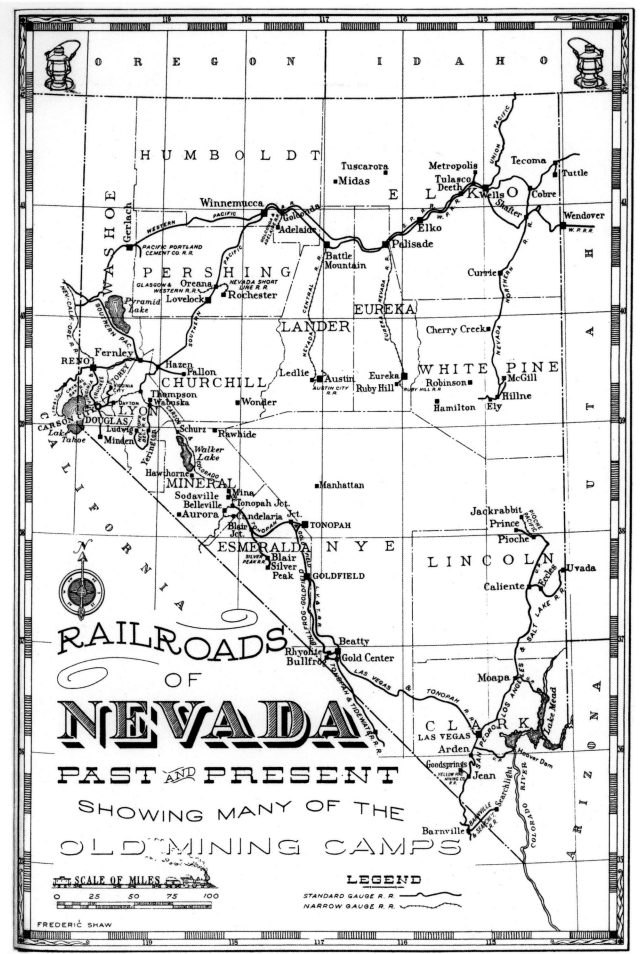

RAILROADS
OF
NEVADA
PAST AND PRESENT
SHOWING MANY OF THE
OLD MINING CAMPS

SCALE OF MILES
0   25   50   75   100

LEGEND
STANDARD GAUGE R. R. ————
NARROW GAUGE R. R. ～～～～

FREDERIC SHAW

Frederic Shaw

SILVER & GOLD

THE SAGEBRUSH NARROW GAUGE operated a hodge-podge of equipment on a shoe string budget for nearly 60 years in a part of the Old West that has been largely overlooked and nearly forgotten.

In the heart of the Great American Basin once ran a most unlikely and historic narrow gauge railway. Built to carry the commerce of rich silver and gold strikes, the Nevada Central (NC) Railway struggled against all odds for six decades.

It all started quite by accident when a Pony Express rider's horse kicked over a chunk of silver-laden rock in 1861. The discovery, in what is now upper Austin's Pony Canyon, started a silver rush. Mining claims were staked out and almost overnight Austin became a wild west town and supply point in the middle of it all.

Following the Civil War, it was hoped that the builders of the Central Pacific would follow the old Pony Express and stage routes through Austin. But, the transcontinental railroad was built 90 miles north through Battle Mountain in order to avoid the central Nevada mountain ranges. Austin and its mines needed their own rail connection. So, beginning in 1879 the NC was built in order to open up this vast and virtually unpopulated area of the Silver State.

BARREN SAGEBRUSH COUNTRY

Running through some of the most barren and remote high desert sagebrush and mountain country in the West, the NC rolled down through the years with much of its original equipment, mainly because it could never afford to purchase anything newer.

The most amazing part of the story is that this little three foot gauge, begun in the late 1870s, not only survived so long, but that many of its original locomotives and cars lasted long enough to be preserved. Not that the NC's owners and builders had any interest in "historic preservation," it was simply that this 93-mile-long "line in the sand" never made enough money to buy more modern equipment.

Hence, the NC steamed and clanked down through the years like some lost tribe.

-Mallory Hope Ferrell

A LINE IN THE SAND

 MY FRIEND, the late artist Mike Pearsall, once remarked, "About the only thing you need to model the Nevada Central is some straight track and a bucket of sand!" While Mike's statement appears on the surface to have been both humorous and correct, there is a great deal more to the NC story.

There were grades, a twisting mountain canyon, rich mines, frequent washouts, obscure feeder railroads and antique equipment that lasted so long as to become rolling museum pieces by the time of the Great Depression.

If the truth be known, the NC operated in its own depression from the 1890s until its demise in 1938. Historian Gilbert Kneiss wrote that the NC was "...a rather humble line, never very profitable and usually struggling along in the red and hoping times would change."

It was not even the first Nevada narrow gauge line to carry the NC name. That honor belonged to another three foot gauge mining railroad at Pioche. The first Nevada Central Railroad, which everyone called the "Pioche & Bullionville," failed at about the same time the "new" NC was getting started.

SILVER DISCOVERED
The NC was incorporated in 1879, a result of rich silver discoveries in the hills around Austin, Nevada. The original motive power and rolling stock all came second- or thirdhand and dated from the early 1870s. However, a few

pieces of new equipment were added after the road opened the following year. Two Baldwin Moguls came in 1881, a result of the mighty Union Pacific taking an interest in the new road. These two 2-6-0s were the only new locomotives to ever run on the road, and they were still around at the end when the NC gave up the ghost.

After the mid-1880s, the silver mines around Austin were an "on again, off again" proposition as old veins played out and new discoveries were made. There were no other towns between the two terminals, and the actual mines were served by a pair of connecting feeders, with their steep grades.

The NC never actually reached downtown Austin City itself, the supply point for area mines and camps. The NC tracks ended at Clifton in the valley a mile below Austin proper. Entry into the Lander County seat was left to the short, steeply-graded Austin City Railway and its *Mules' Relief* steam dummy, which ran up Austin's Main Street to the Manhattan Mill and Lander Hill mines.

GOLD IS FOUND

Soon after the 1880 completion of the Nevada Central, gold ore was discovered at the Morgan Mine in Lewis Canyon, 10 miles east of the new narrow gauge. The following year, the Battle Mountain & Lewis Railroad was constructed from Galena, a station some 10 miles south of Battle Mountain, to the Starr Grove Mill and Lewis Canyon mines.

The 12-mile BM&L utilized five switchbacks, and its new locomotive was found to be incapable of pulling even itself up the steep canyon grade. It was necessary to rent a NC engine to power the line. The BM&L engine was returned to its San Francisco builder and a second, more powerful engine was ordered. The replacement locomotive, named *Starr Grove*, was never delivered as the BM&L was already in financial trouble.

The Lewis Canyon line operated less than a year, when the NC assumed control for back rent on its locomotives and other debts. The NC ran an occasional train to the mines in 1883 and 1885, but thereafter the gold mines shut down and the Lewis railroad lay dormant until dismantled in 1890.

The Nevada Central eventually tried to make ends meet with the purchase of gasoline-powered rail buses to carry the U.S. mail, small packages and the few passengers who wanted to ride. Even these "infernal combustion" machines had a character all their own as they puttered between the Southern Pacific (former Central Pacific) connection at Battle Mountain and Clifton.

In this land of high desert and even higher peaks, there is a great deal to still be discovered, not the least of which is the Nevada Central. This is the story of that unique line.

In the distance, a thin wisp of smoke (opposite page) signals the arrival of a Nevada Central train. Linwood Moody collection
Long out of service, Baldwin Mogul #1 (above) rests and rusts at the Battle Mountain yards in 1938. Richard B. Jackson

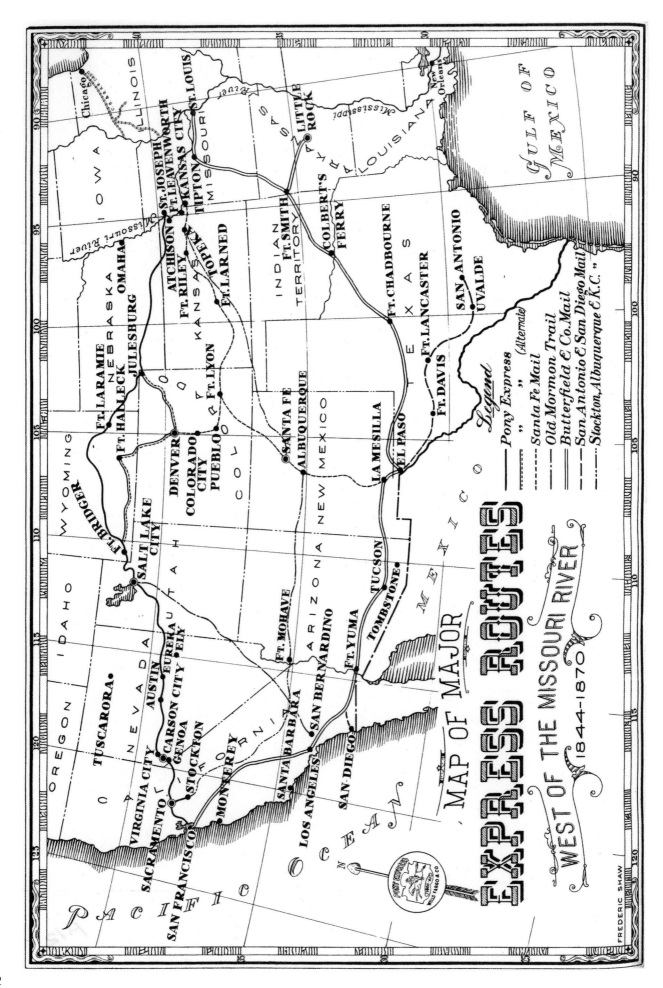

MAP OF MAJOR

EXPRESS ROUTES

WEST OF THE MISSOURI RIVER
1844-1870

Legend

— Pony Express
— " " (Alternate)
— Santa Fe Mail
— Old Mormon Trail
— Butterfield & Co.Mail
— San Antonio & San Diego Mail
— Stockton, Albuquerque & K.C."

FREDERIC SHAW

12

CHAPTER 1
SPURS & SILVER

 THE FAMED PONY EXPRESS operated for only a brief 18 months between April 3, 1860 and October 28, 1861. Young relay riders covered the 1,800 miles between St. Joseph, Missouri and Sacramento, California in 10 days.

An advertisement for express riders called for "young, skinny, wiry fellows not over eighteen. Must be expert riders willing to risk death daily. Orphans preferred." A rider's pay was $25 per month.

The Pony Express route ran through parts of eight states and the desolate sagebrush, mountain and hostile Indian country of Central Nevada. It cost five dollars to mail a half-ounce letter, later reduced to one dollar. Although expensive, it was a decided advantage in time over mail sent "around the horn," or by Wells, Fargo & Company's Concord stage coaches which often required several months.

DOZEN MILE INTERVALS
Stations along the Pony Express and Overland Mail & Stage Company's route were established by owners Russell, Majors & Waddell at roughly 12-mile intervals. Here riders exchanged mounts, without hardly stopping and ate hardtack on the fly. The average express rider rode a 120-mile-roundtrip in about 12 hours, using five horses each way. Riders used Pony Canyon as a shortcut through the 7,484-foot Toiyabe Mountains pass.

Battle Mountain, 90 miles north, was named for an 1857 skirmish between road builders and a band of Shoshones. Central Nevada was still largely unsettled and often dangerous.

Simpson's Park Station was a few miles east of Pony Canyon while Jacobs Spring Station was two miles east of the Reese River. Shoshone Indians attacked and burned the Jacob Spring outpost in the spring of 1860.

On May 20, 1860 another Shoshone band attacked and burned the Simpson's Park Station, murdering Agent James Alcott. Both stations were rebuilt that fall. The express company then hired their own gunfighters to protect the stage coaches carrying emigrants, mail and shipments.

In May 1861, Pony Express rider Bob Haslam's horse kicked loose a piece of highly mineralized ore in what is now Austin's upper Pony Canyon. Jacobs Spring Express Agent William Talcott is said to have sent the ore to Virginia City for assay, and it proved to be rich in silver. The discovery site was named Pony Ledge.

The Pony Express passed through Central Nevada as depicted in the late Frederic Shaw's map of Major Express Routes (opposite page).
A rider passes workers building the telegraph line that replaced the Pony Express (right) after only 18 months of operation. Wells Fargo Bank

A Wells, Fargo & Company stagecoach pauses in front of Carter's Photograph Gallery in Salt Lake City, Utah (above). The rare glass plate negative dates from the 1870s. Author's collection

PONY EXPRESS CLOSES

Four days after the Pacific Telegraph line was completed on October 24, 1861, the Pony Express went out of business. The route continued to be used by the Overland Mail & Stage Company long after the 1869 completion of the transcontinental railroad line.

Miners flocked to the area, and Austin and its mining district were established on July 10, 1862. The town was laid out, and by January 1863 a number of buildings were under construction. Jacobs Spring, now renamed Jacobsville, was declared the county seat, and a courthouse was built there in March 1863. However, the former express station was too far from Lander Hill and the mining activity.

In April 1863, the miners held a meeting and voted to make Austin the Lander County seat. On September 21 the wooden courthouse was moved to Austin and expanded.

Austin grew into a sizable frontier town and within two years was home to some 10,000 souls. It became the second largest city in the Silver State, exceeded only by Virginia City on the Comstock Lode. Ultimately the mines produced more than $50 million in silver and gold and was responsible for the eventual construction of the Nevada Central Railway and its two connecting narrow gauge feeder lines.

When the Central Pacific Railroad built its line through Battle Mountain in 1868, the citizens of Austin began to promote their own rail line to connect with the Central Pacific.

A Pony Express rider races his charge across Central Nevada in a sketch by Paul Nyeland.

LONELIEST ROAD

Today the former Pony Express route is roughly followed by U.S. Highway 50. *Life* magazine described it as the "Loneliest Road in America," adding that "it contained no attractions and no points of interest." How wrong they were! For those who love the wide open spaces, this is a fantastic area, full of rich history with friendly small towns, some interesting ghost towns and "damn few people."

For the historian there is a great deal of interest along this route with its many picturesque old mining towns. Railroads like the Nevada Northern, Eureka & Palisade, NC, Carson & Colorado, Virginia & Truckee, Carson & Tahoe Lumber & Fluming and others are all crossed by Old Route Fifty. On both sides of the former Overland Stage route are forgotten ghost towns like Hamilton, Belmont, Cortez, Rawhide and Berlin.

In this land where cattle outnumber people and wild horses run free, there are many exciting discoveries, not the least of which is the NC's Sagebrush Narrow Gauge.

Although brief-lived, Pony Express riders (top) captured the imagination of the nation and became a symbol of the Wild West. Coaches of the Overland Mail & Stage Company (below) also plied the route and were subject to holdups that forced the stage line to hire its own gunfighters.
Sketches by Jim Scancarelli

Photographs of camels in the American West are rare. This scene was made at Camp Drum, near Wilmington, California in 1863. Camp Drum was the Army's distribution point for supplies to posts throughout the Southwest. Author's collection

CAMELS ON THE FRONTIER

In May of 1856 the sailing ship *Supply* landed at Indianola, Texas with 31 single-hump Arabian dromedaries and a pair of Bactrian double-hump camels for use by the U.S. Army in the Great American Desert. The camels were taken to Fort Tejon where they served on pack trains and military expeditions.

The camels proved to be tough, ornery and smelly characters that frightened horses and mules, often causing Calvary mounts to stampede. By 1861 the "Camel Corps" had increased to 91 animals and was transferred to Fort Fitzgerald, near Los Angeles, in 1862.

A 300-mile "Dromedary Express" briefly carried supplies and mail from Los Angeles to Fort Mojave, Arizona. During the Civil War, Confederate forces captured 54 of the animals, and by 1863 the Army decided the experiment was a failure and sold the camels.

Meanwhile, 40 Bactrians were brought to California in order to haul salt for the Nevada silver mills. Julius Bandmann put 10 of the double-hump camels to work hauling salt, while San Francisco businessman Otto Esche used 30 of the animals between the Columbus and Rhodes salt marshes, south of Walker Lake, to silver mills near Virginia City.

AUSTIN CAMEL TRAIN

On August 26, 1864, a camel train arrived at the new silver camp of Austin. Wagon loads of salt had cost $120 per ton, while camel-haulage lowered the price to $80. A camel could pack 800 to 1,000 pounds, twice as much as a mule. Another benefit was the fact that camels could forage on almost anything from sage to greasewood and were even known to eat discarded playing cards.

Camel trains continued to haul salt and supplies from Virginia City to Austin for the next few years. However, public outrage in newspapers like Mark Twain's *Territorial Enterprise* began a campaign to outlaw the stubborn, smelly and often uncontrollable dromedaries from public streets and roads. As a result, the Nevada legislature effectively banned camel use in 1876.

Some of the animals were taken to Arizona and British Columbia, but most were simply set free. Over the next few decades, desert travelers and prospectors reported occasional sightings of camels in remote areas. A group of 16 wild camels were spotted in the Goldfield area, near Silver Bow, Nevada in 1905. A herd of 20 was seen in the desert near Penelas as late as 1936.

As late as World War II, occasional sightings were made from time to time. Eventually the camels appear to have perished from a combination of the elements and predators.

Today the "Camel Corps" is but a footnote in the legends of the American West.

A camel train brings salt and other supplies to the Austin mines in 1864. Salt was used to process the newly-discovered rich silver ores. Sketch by Paul Nyeland

Central Pacific Railroad workers lay tracks across the desert near Battle Mountain in 1868. Both anglo and Chinese workmen were employed in the effort. Battle Mountain was some 93 miles north of the silver strikes on Austin's Lander Hill. Alfred Hart

This 1870 annual pass (left) is signed by Central Pacific President Collis P. Huntington. Author's collection

CHAPTER 2
IRON RAILS & SILVER DREAMS

WHEN THE CENTRAL PACIFIC'S transcontinental railroad was constructed through Battle Mountain in 1868, the citizens of Austin began to agitate for a railroad of their own. By 1874 the silver camp was the second largest city in the state. Only Virginia City on the Comstock was larger.

In 1873 a bill for the proposed 90-mile railroad was vetoed by Nevada Governor L. R. Bradley, citing insufficient security. The governor was not a railroad proponent. However, on February 9, 1875, newly-elected State Senator Michael J. Farrell was successful in obtaining approval for a $200,000 county bond from the legislature, over the objections of the governor. There was one major stipulation to the subsidy: the railroad must be completed in five years. Locals began to refer to the proposed railway project as "Farrell's Folly," and felt he had little chance of building the line.

Farrell, who was also secretary of the Manhattan Silver Mining Company and Lander County clerk, had difficulty finding investors in the project. Several years passed, and Austin was booming as new silver and gold camps were springing up throughout the Reese River Mining District.

Colonel Lyman Bridges, a Chicago engineer, became interested in the projected railroad and went west to investigate. Bridges felt the railroad would be a profitable undertaking.

A meeting was held on March 25, 1878 at the Baldwin Hotel in San Francisco, and the Nevada Railway was organized. It would be built from the Central Pacific's depot at Battle Mountain along the Reese River to Austin, a distance estimated to be "about 90 miles."

A Central Pacific passenger train arrives at Battle Mountain, an early meal stop, in an 1869 engraving. Eastbound Train #1 traveled 522 miles from San Francisco and was due at 11:45 a.m. Westbound Train #2 was due at 1:05 p.m., after having traveled 1,391 miles since leaving Omaha. SP collection

THE ARRIVAL AT BATTLE MOUNTAIN STATION, ON THE C. P. R. R.

The crew of an "Emigrant Train" pauses in front of CP's Globe-built 4-4-0 #124 at Mill City, Nevada in 1883. Author's collection

SENATOR FAVORS LINE

Newly-elected State Senator Mike Farrell was convinced that the new line should be built to three foot gauge. In the 1860s he had prospected and staked out mining claims on Ruby Hill near Eureka. He was aware that a similar 90-mile-long narrow gauge line, the Eureka & Palisade Railroad, had been successfully completed in1875 through almost the same type of Nevada terrain.

By July 1878 the Nevada Railway had been completely staked out by Colonel Bridges, but there was still the matter of insufficient funds. Allen Curtis, a director of the railway and superintendent of the Manhattan Silver Mining Company, was unable to obtain enough financing for the railroad even though he also owned the Austin Bank. To moneybags back east, central Nevada was thought of as barren, isolated, and lost somewhere in the "Great American Desert."

On August 27, 1879 a new company was formed under the Nevada Central Railway name. Anson Phelps Stokes, grandson of Anson Greene Phelps— founder of Phelps Dodge and a major Phelps Dodge stockholder— became interested in controlling the Central Nevada silver mines. Phelps already had an interest in Austin's Manhattan Silver Mining Company.

Stokes wanted to consolidate and develop Nevada's silver mines much like Phelps Dodge had done with the copper mines of Arizona. He also wanted a rail connection for his Manhattan Silver Mine and Mill.

With Stokes' backing the railroad could now be built. Early on the morning of September 15, 1879, a meeting was held at the Capitol Hotel in Battle Mountain. The new Nevada Central Railway was organized with essentially the same principals, plus Anson Stokes, as the earlier Nevada Railway. Surveys and other assets of the Nevada Railway, amounting to $8,938.58, were transferred to the new railroad. Less than 18 months remained to claim the Lander County bond monies, and time was running out.

Officers of the new railway were: W.S. Gage, President, San Francisco, California; R.L.S. Hall, Vice President, New York City, New York; A.A. Curtis, Treasurer, Austin, Nevada; J.D. Negus, Secretary, Battle Mountain, Nevada; Lyman Bridges, Chief Engineer, Chicago, Illinois; J.C. Fisher, Master Mechanic, Battle Mountain, Nevada; F.W. Dunn, Assistant Supt., Battle Mountain, Nevada.

Members of the Board of Directors were D.B. Hatch, New York City, New York; M.E. Angel, Battle Mountain, Nevada; James H. Ledlie, Utica, New York; M.J. Farrell, Austin, Nevada; and A. Nichols, Austin, Nevada.

THE FIRST NEVADA CENTRAL

The Nevada Central Railway of 1879 was the second Nevada narrow gauge to carry this name. Years earlier, in 1873, General A. L. Page and other mining men built a three-foot-gauge railway between Pioche and Bullionville, about 20 miles. Originally incorporated in 1872 as the Pioche & Bullionville Railroad, it began operation under the Nevada Central Railroad herald on June 8, 1873. Its main source of traffic was gold ore from the mines around Pioche (pop. 7,500 in 1872) to the mills at Bullionville (pop. 450).

Soon after the first Nevada Central was completed, mining began a decline due to exhaustion of high grade ores and complications of underground water in the deeper mines. Regular operations ceased in 1878, and the bankrupt little line's assets were sold by the county sheriff at Pioche on March 3, 1881.

NEW BRANCH BUILT

Some of the original NCRR equipment as well as portions of its grade were utilized along Treasure Hill at Pioche in early January 1890. This operation was extended to about three miles in length, and a new 15-mile branch was built to the Jackrabbit Mine northwest of Pioche, at Royal (Bristol). The mining line was incorporated as the Pioche Pacific Transportation Co. in 1891, and narrow gauge operations continued until 1948.

Today, one of the P&P's locomotives, a 2-6-0, is displayed beside the county courthouse in Pioche, while a small Shay is in private hands and under restoration in Washington state.

The Pioche & Bullionville Railroad, incorporated in 1872, began operations as the (first) NC Railroad in 1873. Its three-foot-gauge Grant-built 2-6-0 *Colonel J.F. Carter* sits atop a trestle at the Bullionville gold mill in the mid-1870s. Lincoln County Museum

Nevada Central 4-4-0 #5 with mixed train, crew, agent and passengers awaits departure from Battle Mountain depot in about 1885. The trim Baldwin came to the NC in early 1881 from the North Pacific Coast, where it had been named *Sonoma.* Author's collection

CHAPTER 3

RAILS THROUGH THE SAGE

 WITH THE BACKING OF ANSON STOKES, the first mile of grade was reported to have been finished on September 13, 1879. The *Battle Mountain Messenger* noted that, "No contracts have been awarded as General J. H. Ledlie, the contractor and Mr. M.E. Angel are still west and due back today." Little more than four months remained to build more than 90 miles of railroad. Otherwise the $200,000 in county bonds would be lost.

Five days after the September 15, 1879 organizational meeting at Battle Mountain's Capitol Hotel, the Nevada Central Railway's newly-appointed Chief Engineer, Lyman Bridges, awarded a grading contract for the first 80 miles to McGregor and Blossom. The grading was to be completed within 60 days. The contractor placed advertisements for 500 workers in newspapers throughout the West.

EXCAVATORS TO HELP

At the same time, M. N. Mason, superintendent of the Grade Manufacturing Company, arranged to ship a dozen "New Era Railway Excavators" from Chicago. These animal-powered scrapers were said to be capable of building two miles of grade per day on flat terrain.

The Battle Mountain paper reported on September 13 that the first mile of grade was completed, and that General J. H. Ledlie, the NC's contractor, was "still out West." Ledlie was buying rails and equipment for the new narrow gauge.

The September 1879 trips "out West" by General Ledlie, Angel, and Colonel Bridges involved the purchase of large quantities of rail and equipment from two ill-fated California narrow gauge lines. These acquisitions would provide the basic materials, locomotives, rolling stock and other items for initial construction and operation of the Nevada Central Railway. Some of these items would still be in use 60 years later.

RAILROAD TO BATTLE MOUNTAIN

The entire Monterey & Salinas Valley Railroad would be sent "lock, stock and barrel" to Battle Mountain. The equipment consisted of two Baldwin locomotives, a 4-4-0 and a 2-6-0, two combination passenger cars, eight box cars, 40 flatcars, a pair of "iron cars" (heavy-duty flats), two handcars, two gallows turntables, several water tanks and more than 38 miles of rail. The rolling stock had all been constructed on site in 1874 by Thomas Carter, prior to the formation of the well-known Carter Brothers car building firm.

The Monterey & Salinas Valley had been built by local wheat farmers in 1874 in order to provide an economical alternative to high freight rates charged by the Southern Pacific. It was the first narrow gauge common carrier in the Golden State. However, by mid-1875 the little road was losing money and was sold by the Monterey County Sheriff to the Pacific Improvement Company, which had been organized by the Southern Pacific. Sales price was $128,558 or roughly one-third of its original cost.

The Southern Pacific had little use for the lightly-built three-foot M&SV as it was building their own standard gauge line from Castroville Junction, bypassing all but about 10 miles of the old narrow gauge grade northeast of Monterey. The SP was already in contact with the NC, and on October 19, 1879 the NC agreed to the purchase. The *Battle Mountain Messenger* reported that one locomotive and a passenger car are "already on their way."

Also on October 19, 1879 the NC's Board of Directors approved the purchase of 150 tons of new, unused rail and rolling stock of the proposed Stockton & Ione Railroad. The equipment was reported to include three boxcars, a "combination" (caboose?) car and the redwood frame for a passenger car, all believed to have been constructed by the Holt Brothers in 1875-76. The NC sent Richard Amerman to Stockton to oversee loading and shipping.

EQUIPMENT ARRIVES

Throughout the autumn of 1879, large quantities of 35-pound iron rails, ties, rolling stock and two interesting locomotives began arriving. The Battle Mountain newspaper reported on October 4 that construction materials were piling up near the depot and "an engine and 20 cars are due Monday, when track laying will begin in earnest." However, these flat cars and locomotive were not from the recently-purchased Monterey & Salinas Valley nor the Stockton & Ione.

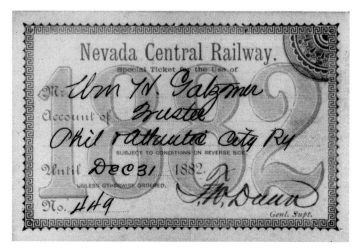

A rare early Nevada Central Railway pass.
Author's collection

NC'S FIRST TWO LOCOMOTIVES

The identity and origin of the Nevada Central's first two locomotives have been a point of conjecture and discussion among historians for well over a half-century. Careful research into existing records and contemporary newspaper reports has helped to correct some previous well-meaning assumptions that proved to be inaccurate.

The locomotives, mentioned by the *Battle Mountain Messenger* in the October 4, 1879 edition, were from an entirely different source "back East." The Bath & Hammondsport Railroad in western New York state had converted to standard gauge and the *Hammondsport Herald* reported on September 24, 1879 that their 2-6-0 *Jonathan Robie* had been "sold to a Western party." The *Jonathan Robie* (Brooks c/n 230-1875) was identical to the *Kate Connor* (Brooks c/n 167-1873) of the Salt Lake, Sevier Valley & Pioche Railroad, with which it has previously been confused.

On September 24, 1879 the *Reese River Reveille* reported that "an engine will arrive from the East this week." Two days later the *Silver State* of Winnemucca stated that "a locomotive and cars are expected from the East in a week or two." The *Battle Mountain Messenger* gave a few more details a week later, saying that, "Twenty cars and a locomotive, for the Nevada Central Railway, passed through Cheyenne several days ago, and are about due at Battle Mountain."

Superintendent of Construction R. M. Steele unloaded the engine and 20 cars on October 4. The new 2-6-0 would become NC #1, the *Battle Mountain*, and would be used initially in construction train service.

PURCHASE E&P CARS

On October 3, 1879 the Nevada Central purchased a locomotive and 10 cars from the nearby Eureka & Palisade. This equipment arrived four days later. The engine was a small Mason Fairlie 0-4-4 that had been E&P's #1, the *Eureka*. On the NC, she was named *Austin* and numbered 2, although generally referred to simply as "the Dinky."

Nevada Central workers wasted no time in getting the Mason steamed up. Although she was reported to have "leaked badly," the *Austin* (#2) was put in service on October 8, 1879. The NC was the third railroad this engine would help build. It was the first engine under steam on the NC and had quite an interesting history before arriving in Battle Mountain.

Constructed in 1871 (c/n 461), it was William Mason's first narrow gauge locomotive and first Mason Bogie. The engine was so unique that even before being completed at the Taunton, Massachusetts works, the *Railroad Gazette* ran a story and an engraving of the *Onward* in its November 25, 1871 issue.

In 1872 the little *Onward* was sold to the American Fork R.R. in Utah, where it was renamed *American Fork*. Despite conflicting reports of its success, the engine was soon sidelined due to mechanical problems. It was replaced by horse power on the steep, twisting little mining railroad, until a new Porter Bell & Co. 0-6-0 tender engine arrived in 1874.

The "Mason Bogie" was sold again in late 1873, becoming the first locomotive of the abuilding Eureka & Palisade R.R., where she was named *Eureka*. Replaced by newer and larger power on the E&P, the little Fairlie was sold to the NC in 1879. It is interesting to note that after serving the NC, the *Austin* would be sold yet another time to operate on another Western narrow gauge road, the Utah & Northern.

Bath & Hammondsport RR *Jonathan Robie*, a Brooks 2-6-0, waits at the Hammondsport, New York dock, with steamer *Lulu* in 1878-79. This engine became the Nevada Central's *Battle Mountain*, (first) #1 in 1879. Clare R.J. Rogers collection

Brooks-built *Kate Connor* 2-6-0 (c/n167-1873) of the Salt Lake, Sevier Valley & Pioche Railroad (below) has been incorrectly listed in published works as having gone to the Nevada Central. However, an identical Brooks Mogul (c/n 230-1875) from the Bath & Hammondsport Railroad in New York became the NC (first) #1 *Battle Mountain*. The *Kate Connor* remained in Utah and is shown (above) in service on the Utah Western Railway near Salt Lake City. Author's collection and C.R. Savage

Nevada Central's second locomotive was Mason Locomotive & Machine Works' first "Bogie." The *Onward* was built on speculation in 1871 and sold to the American Fork R.R. (1872) before going to the Eureka & Palisade R.R. in 1874. She became NC's *Austin* #2 in 1879 and was later on the Utah & Northern (UP). Her builder's photo (above) and steel engraving (below) show **minor variations.** Art Wallace and author's collection

CONSTRUCTION GETS UNDER WAY

By October 25, McGregor & Blossom's crews had completed 30 miles of grade, and R. M. Steele's track layers had put down 15 miles of ties and rail. The Nevada Central paid the Central Pacific $9,207.57 in freight charges that month. Some 350 men and 300 horses and mules were strung along the grade.

The *Battle Mountain* Mogul and Mason Bogie *Austin* were hard pressed to keep up with demand as more rails and rolling stock arrived. The first freight train was sent to "end of track" on November 3. It carried supplies and equipment for the Manhattan Silver Mining Co., lumber, and merchandise for Gage & Curtis in Austin. Wagons forwarded the shipment the rest of the way.

Locomotive #3, a former M&SV 2-6-0, arrived on December 27, 1879 and was promptly named *Anson P. Stokes*. The 1874 Baldwin was soon put in service to help the other two engines.

Milepost 40 was reached by January 2, 1880, and W. N. Mason, builder of the celebrated grading and ditching machines, returned to Chicago, satisfied with the success of his invention. Grading soon reached the Reese River Stage Station, near Vaughns (Milepost 62) and rails were in as far as Hot Springs (Milepost 35). Track gangs were spiking down an average of two miles each day, with little more than a month to go in order to claim the Lander County bond funds.

A telegraph line was constructed next to the right-of-way, and the NC began running Combine #1 behind the daily construction train. Conductor Charlie Benson found the former M&SV car to "work like a charm."

Nevada Central contractor John A. Blossom

NEW TANK ERECTED

Back at Battle Mountain, the enginehouse and machine shop were almost finished, and the narrow gauge was erecting a new water tank. Previously, the NC was forced to lay a trough from the CP's tank in order to fill its engines. Tracks were now laid past Bobtown, 50 miles south of Battle Mountain.

Sixteen carloads of iron, six more flatcars and another locomotive arrived on Friday night, January 16. In addition to rails acquired from the Monterey & Salinas Valley and Stockton & Ione, the NC purchased nine carloads of rail from the Pacific Rolling Mills in San Francisco. These arrived on January 10, 1880.

The former M&SV Baldwin 4-4-0 became NC #4 and was named for the road's new Vice President D. B. Hatch. The locomotive was set up and made its first trip on January 23, 1880. Three days later NC #5, the *General Ledlie* made a trial trip. This trim Baldwin 4-4-0 had been built in 1876 as the North Pacific Coast's *Sonoma* #12. On the NC it soon had a painted star on its numberplate.

The NC obtained the rails and rolling stock of the never-built Stockton & Ione RR in 1879. However, the NC did not obtain the beautiful Mason Bogie *Stockton* which was returned to the builder, rebuilt as an 0-4-6 and resold to the 42" gauge Covington, Columbus & Black Hills. Author's collection

MYTHS AND LEGENDS

By January 24 grading was complete except for one mile between Marshall Canyon and Clifton. Grading contractors McGregor & Blossom dissolved their partnership, and J. A. Blossom stayed on to finish the job. The NC's payroll reached $40,000 by month's end. A new coach shed and coal house were under construction near the Battle Mountain shops, and the second former M&SV combination car arrived from California.

Tracks were in place some 77 miles (south of Silver Creek) by January 31. With only little more than a week to go, construction ran at a feverish pace as the work trains rushed rails, ties, supplies and carloads of hay for the animals to "the front." The telegraph line was almost complete. Conductor Charlie Benson was made dispatcher at Austin in order to keep trains in order, on schedule and avoid sagebrush head-ons.

By 3:00 p.m. on Saturday, February 7, 1880, four and a half miles of track remained to be laid between Ledlie and Clifton. With only 33 hours remaining for the franchise, the Nevada Central was cutting it pretty close!

The story of the Nevada Central's next few hours have become part of the myths and legends of the Old West. The facts, however do not support many of the wild stories. The NC's last mile is an interesting story in itself. Too bad the colorful tales and myths aren't true.

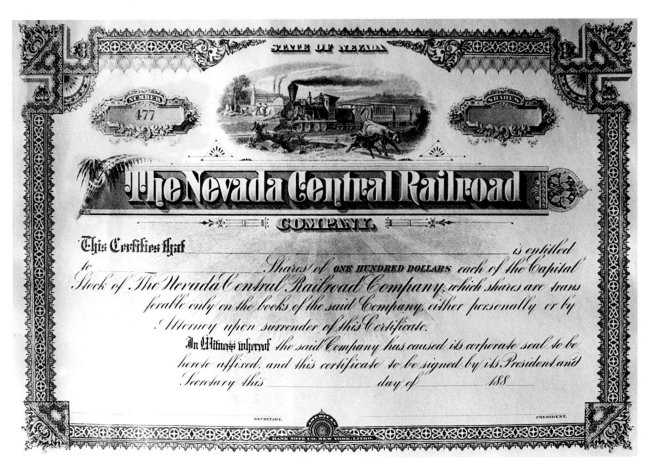

Ward Kimball collection

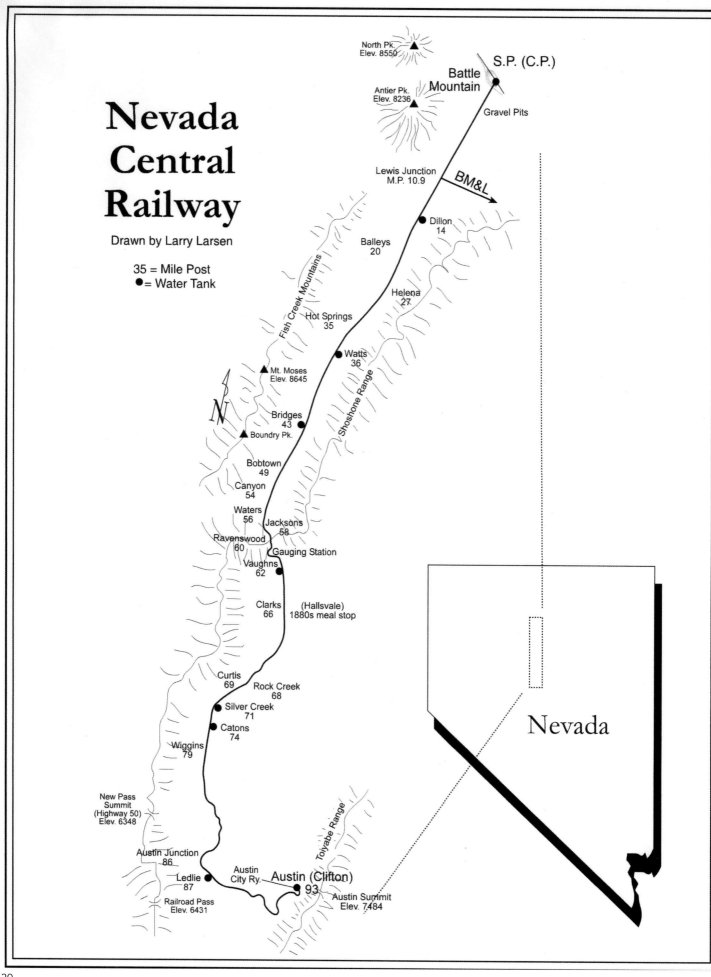

Nevada Central Railway

Drawn by Larry Larsen

35 = Mile Post
●= Water Tank

North Pk.
Elev. 8550

S.P. (C.P.)

Battle
Mountain

Antier Pk.
Elev. 8236

Gravel Pits

Lewis Junction
M.P. 10.9

BM&L

Dillon
14

Balleys
20

Fish Creek Mountains

Helena
27

Hot Springs
35

Watts
36

Shoshone Range

Mt. Moses
Elev. 8645

N

Bridges
43

Boundry Pk.

Bobtown
49

Canyon
54

Waters
56

Jacksons
58

Ravenswood
60

Gauging Station

Vaughns
62

Clarks
66

(Hallsvale)
1880s meal stop

Curtis
69

Rock Creek
68

Silver Creek
71

Catons
74

Wiggins
79

New Pass
Summit
(Highway 50)
Elev. 6348

Toiyabe Range

Austin Junction
86

Ledlie
87

Austin
City Ry.

Austin (Clifton)
93

Railroad Pass
Elev. 6431

Austin Summit
Elev. 7484

Nevada

CHAPTER 4
SILVER STRIKES AT MIDNIGHT

OVER THE LAST CENTURY, many articles and history books have repeated the story of the Austin City limits being extended just before midnight so that the Nevada Central would receive its Lander County bonds.

The 1949 20th Century-Fox motion picture *A Ticket To Tomahawk* capitalized on this scenario of expanding the limits of the factious Colorado town of Tomahawk in order for the narrow gauge Tomahawk & Western to claim its subsidy. It makes a great story but is not supported by the facts.

The real story of the final hours leading up to the completion of the Nevada Central is just as exciting as the often-told myth. Contemporary newspapers recorded the actual events.

By January 31, 1880, with only nine days remaining to complete the railroad and claim a $200,000 subsidy, track crews were working just south of Silver Creek, at Milepost 77, with over 16 miles to go. By Saturday February 7, there still remained four and a half miles of rail to be laid. However, the supply of 35-pound iron and crossties was running short at the end of track, known as "the front."

The often-repeated story of the Austin City limits being extended just before midnight on February 9, 1880 has no basis in fact. The NC's tracks reached their destination of Clifton at 10 minutes before midnight, just in time to qualify for the Lander County bonds. Three silver-plated spikes were driven, followed by speeches and a torch-light parade. Artist Paul Nyeland depicted the scene.

THE LAST DAY

On Monday morning, February 9, 1880, the last day, it looked as though the task would not be finished in time. Steele's track crews were nearly out of rail, and the supply train that had left Battle Mountain the day before had not yet arrived. Dawn brought warmer weather as the delayed supply train, with 16 loads of rail and ties, came into sight behind the knoll below Tucker's Ranch.

The platform cars were unloaded, and by nightfall only about a mile of track remained to reach the Austin City boundary line below town at Clifton. With six hours to go, R.M. Steele knew his men could beat the deadline.

Bonfires had been built along the right-of-way, and ties had been laid during the day. The workers had developed a clockwork routine as one group placed the rails, while another gauged and pounded the spikes in the light of torches and fires. Townspeople came down the hill from Austin to watch the activity.

At 10 minutes before midnight, the tracks were in place 900 feet inside the city limits. Allen Curtis presented General Ledlie and Colonel Bridges with silver-plated spikes, which they each "drove home" to accompanying cheers from the crowd.

A third spike was driven by Curtis, the Nevada Central's treasurer, in honor of Anson Stokes of the syndicate that financed the road. Brief speeches were made by Bridges and Ledlie announcing that the "feat had been accomplished." A sky rocket was shot into the air, as a signal for the firing of two canons on opposite hillsides overlooking Pony Canyon. It was a successful photo finish at the Austin City limits.

A torchlight parade marched down Austin's Main Street that was lit by more bonfires, rockets and Roman Candles. The *Reese River Reveille* reported that at 2:00 a.m. it was "as bright as day."

NO BOUNDARY EXTENSION

The *Battle Mountain Messenger's* extensive coverage of the event makes no mention of any last-minute boundary extension. Likewise, nothing has ever been found in the official Lander County Court House records. Long-time County Recorder Bert Acre searched for years in an effort to confirm or deny the city limits story and concluded that it just simply was the result of an "old wives' tale."

The very next day after the silver spike celebrations, a thunderstorm caused washouts and damaged the Nevada Central's freshly-laid, unballasted trackage. In haste, some tracks had been laid directly on frozen ground. Although built across an arid, high desert profile, washouts and flash floods would plague the NC throughout its lifetime.

The contractor began running through trains on February 24, 1880. Regular passenger and freight service did not begin until March 1, the same day the telegraph line was finished.

The schedule called for an eight hour and 20 minute trip from Battle Mountain to Clifton, where stages took passengers one mile up the hill to Austin. One way fare was $9.00. Intermediate fares between stations were 10 cents per mile, and freight was carried at one cent per mile/per hundred weight.

A meal stop was established northbound at Bridges (M.P. 43) and at Hallsvale (M.P. 66) for southbound passengers. Hallsvale was soon renamed Clarks. The entire 93-mile run averaged only about 11 miles per hour, with a five mile per hour restriction over switches until the road-bed had settled.

Carpenters were busy rebuilding the platform on the south side of the CP's Battle Mountain depot, lowering it by two feet to accommodate the narrow gauge's smaller equipment. On March 1, 1880 the Nevada Central's Cashier Richard Amerman received a new four-ton Hall & Company safe. The line's operations were already showing a profit.

FIRES HIT RAILROAD

On March 3, a fire that started in Battle Mountain's Central Pacific freighthouse, spread to the nearby Capital Hotel and Wells Fargo office, destroying both structures. At the same time, a fire which broke out in the Nevada Central's enginehouse and machine shop was quickly extinguished before any major damage was done. Arson by disgruntled construction workers, about to lose their jobs, was suspected, although nothing was ever proven.

With completion of the Clifton depot, enginehouse and gallows turntable in early March, some 60 carpenters and laborers were discharged and given tickets back to San Francisco. On March 16, 1880 the NC was awarded a contract to carry the U.S. Mail. Wells Fargo & Company express also rode the new slim gauge rails.

A Nevada Central roster published on March 15, 1880 showed the following equipment in service: 3 wood burning locomotives, 2 combination passenger cars, 45 flat cars, 17 boxcars and 11 hand (pump) cars. This listing obviously did not include 4-4-0s *D. B. Hatch* (#4) and *General Ledlie* (#5) which had arrived on the property in mid-January.

The road was reorganized on May 1, 1880 with the following officers and directors: Joseph Collett, president; Robert S. Walker, vice president; D. B. Hatch, treasurer; Anson P. Stokes, Allen A. Curtis, Michael J. Farrell and Andrew Nichols.

Operating personnel included Joseph Collett, general manager; F. W. Dunn, superintendent; C. W. Hinchcliffe, general freight agent, and Richard Amerman, cashier.

NINETY-THREE MILES LONG

As constructed, the NC boasted 93 miles of 35-pound iron rail, curves varied between 6 to 22 degrees, six miles of 2% grade near Austin (115 feet per mile), and the total cost was $944,590.58.

The Capital Hotel in Battle Mountain was rebuilt, and its grand opening was the occasion for the NC's first excursion. Fare for the roundtrip to Austin and back was $5.00.

As soon as the tracks were aligned, leveled and dirt-ballasted, the scheduled time for the daily passenger train was greatly reduced.

An interesting note in the *Battle Mountain Messenger* of September 15, 1880 stated, "The Nevada Central locomotives are burning wood again." This seems to indicate that they were previously burning coal.

The *Revielle* reported on October 20, 1880, under the heading "Engines And Cars Sold," that NC locomotives #1 and #3 along with 10 flatcars and a caboose had been sold to the Utah Eastern Railroad. This sale included the 1875 Brooks Mogul *Battle Mountain* and the 1874 Baldwin 2-6-0 *Anson P. Stokes*. This was the first mention of an early caboose on the NC.

By December, the shop crew was finishing a "neat and substantial" caboose, fitted up with seats, closets and painted red. The shop boys said that it can be seen "40 miles away" and is "an offspring of the old black caboose."

Connections were made at Austin Junction (M.P. 86), later named Ledlie, with Traynor's Fast Freight teams for "All Points in Southern Nevada." At Austin, stage coaches ran to the mining camps of Ione, Grantsville, Cloverdale, Candelaria, Columbus, Belleville, Gold Mountain, Silver Peak, Belmont, Kingston and the other "southern mines." It was at this time that the Nevada Central Railway began advertising itself as the "Austin Route, the shortest and quickest to all points in Central and Southern Nevada." They added that by taking the NC, "Passengers can avoid the long and tedious stage routes."

TRAIN SCHEDULES

By 1881, Train #1 left Battle Mountain's Central Pacific connection at 4:55 p.m. daily and arrived in Austin at 10:40 each evening, requiring only 5:45 hours enroute. Northbound Train #2 left Austin each morning at 5:00 and pulled into Battle Mountain at 10:30 a.m. Southbound trains ran downgrade and required a quarter hour less time. The tri-weekly freight train averaged 10 loads, plus Less than Carload (LCL) freight and express shipments carried aboard one of the combines.

Business on the new narrow gauge was booming. However, the glory days were all too brief. By the spring of 1881, the Carson & Colorado Railroad had been finished between Mound House on the Virginia & Truckee and Hawthorne. It provided a shorter route to some of the southern mining camps. Almost overnight, business on the NC fell off. Soon, freight and passengers were able to reach Belleville and Candelaria over an all-rail route via the Virginia & Truckee and Carson & Colorado railroads, thus avoiding a bumpy stage coach ride altogether.

Traffic on the NC "boomed" soon after the line was finished in 1880. In the spring of 1881, the Carson & Colorado Railroad was completed from Mound House on the Virginia & Truckee to Hawthorne, Nevada. The C&C provided a shorter route to the "southern mines" and took some of the business away from the NC. A C&C mixed train is about to depart from Mound House in 1882. The UN-Reno Library

The narrow gauge Carson & Colorado RR was the Nevada Central's major competitor for traffic to and from the mining camps of Central and Southern Nevada. Traynor's Fast Freight wagons and stagecoaches connected with NC trains at Austin Junction (Ledlie), running to Grantsville, Ione, Candelaria, Silver Peak, Belmont and other "southern mining camps." However, supplies and passengers were soon able to reach Belleville and Candelaria on an all-rail route over the Virginia & Truckee and Carson & Colorado, thus avoiding a dusty stagecoach ride altogether.

An early C&C construction train (left) sits on freshly-laid track near Hawthorne in 1881. A C&C 4-4-0 heads an ore train across a trestle (below) on the Candelaria Branch in c.1885. Author's collection

FROM HEEL TO HERO

Nevada Central's Chief Engineer James Hewitt Ledlie was hailed as the driving force in building the Nevada Central narrow gauge. However, he had a past that labeled him a coward.

The Utica, New York native was a Major in the Third New York Artillery when the Civil War broke out in the spring of 1861. Three years later he became a Brigadier General, under General Ambrose Burnside's IX Corps, of the Army of the Potomac.

During the Battle of Petersburg, a rail center south of the Confederate capital of Richmond, Virginia, in June 1864, Union forces under General Grant sustained heavy losses, and the battle turned into a long stalemate, with neither side advancing. Former coal miners from the 48th Pennsylvania began digging a 510-foot-long tunnel under Southern fortifications.

The excavation was completed on July 23 and filled with four tons of gunpowder. The plan of attack called for General Ledlie to lead his men during the first wave, following the detonation of the explosives.

At 4:40 a.m. the morning of July 26 an explosion rocked the rebel breastworks beneath portions of the 18th and 22nd South Carolina defenders. A crater some 170 feet long and 80 feet deep was created, and 12,000 Union Army soldiers charged into the smoking pit. However, General Ledlie was not leading his troops, who were then fired down upon by Confederate riflemen, who said, "It was like shooting fish in a barrel." The Confederate General opposing Ledlie's troops was William Mahone, who would later build the Norfolk & Western Railway.

Hundreds of Union troops died, and more than 1,400 were captured. Ledlie and fellow General Edward Ferrero, commander of the 4th Division, had been drinking all night in a tent and were either unable or unwilling to take charge of the attack, which without leadership had turned into a military disaster.

RESIGNS COMMISSION

Ledlie resigned his commission in disgrace and headed west. He eventually found work as an engineer and obtained a contract to build trestles and bridges for the Union Pacific's transcontinental railroad.

In 1879 Ledlie was instrumental in obtaining the financial backing of Anson Phelps Stokes in order to build the Nevada Central, for which he became a director and the road's contractor.

The settlement of Austin Junction, seven miles south of Austin, was renamed Ledlie in his honor. It was a freighting station on the Nevada Central, with wagons going to Candelaria, Ione, Belmont and Silver Peak. General Ledlie died on August 2, 1882, having regained the respect of all associated with the Sagebrush Narrow Gauge. After 1900 the settlement of Ledlie became a supply point for brief-lived mining camps at Skookum (1906-09) and New Pass (1917-1920). Today, only a single small building remains at the townsite.

Nevada Central's 4-4-0 #5 came to the road in January 1880 and was named *Gen'l J.H. Ledlie*. Baldwin built it in 1876 as *North Pacific Coast Sonoma* #12. Following a rebuilding in October 1880 the engine was renamed *Jos. Collett* in honor of the line's general manager. A painted star adorns its numberplate as it poses with the crew at Battle Mountain, coupled to a taper-sill open stock car. The UN-Reno Library

NC's *Gen'l J.H. Ledlie* #5 waits at the Battle Mountain Depot in 1880. The 4-4-0 carries the number 12 on its "spot plate" from her North Pacific Coast days. A Central Pacific passenger train waits in the background. J.H Crockwell-Gilbert Kneiss collection

CHAPTER 5

UNION PACIFIC TAKES OVER

SOON AFTER THE NEVADA CENTRAL was finished, Anson Phelps Stokes made plans for two new narrow gauge extensions for his "Austin Route." The Nevada Southern Railroad and the Nevada Northern Railroad were both organized on February 25, 1880 to build narrow gauge connections north and south from the NC. The officers and directors were essentially the same men involved with the Nevada Central. Lyman Bridges served as chief engineer for both lines.

According to *Poor's Manual* for 1880, the Nevada Southern RR would build from Ledlie station on the NC, south to Cloverdale, a distance of 80 miles. James H. Ledlie was president, Andrew Nichols served as vice president and R.L.S. Hall was treasurer. Following a reorganization of NC officers and directors on May 1, 1880, the Nevada Southern's Articles of Incorporation were filed with the state on November 6, 1880, listing a different slate of officers: Joseph Collett, president; Anson P. Stokes, vice president; and C.W. Hinchcliffe was secretary.

The Nevada Northern RR was projected 120 miles north from Battle Mountain to the Idaho line and eventually to the Snake River in Oregon. R.L.S. Hall was president and treasurer, and J.D. Negus was secretary. This proposed railroad should not be confused with the later standard gauge line with the same name that was built between the copper mines at Ely, Nevada and the Southern Pacific in the early 1900s.

LOCATION TEAM SURVEYS

On March 3, 1880, a location team under J.R. Hudson was in the field making surveys for the Nevada Northern. Newspapers indicated it would be built in cooperation with the Central Pacific.

Although a *Reese River Reveille* editorial about the proposed extensions said there was "nothing in it," some grading was said to have been accomplished on the Nevada Southern.

Business was booming on the new railroad, with silver and gold strikes reported weekly in central Nevada and the "southern mines." The NC entered an order for two new Moguls with the Baldwin Locomotive Works in Philadelphia on August 20, 1880. These 2-6-0s were to be numbered (second) #1 and #2 and were delivered in the spring of 1881. They would be the only new locomotives to ever serve the Sagebrush Narrow Gauge.

Meanwhile, the NC was able to sell 1875 Brooks 2-6-0 #1 *Battle Mountain* and 1874 Baldwin 2-6-0 #3 *Anson P. Stokes*, along with 10 flat cars and a caboose to the Utah Eastern in December of 1880. The Brooks-built #1 was one of the very first locomotives to arrive on the NC and came from the Bath & Hammondsport in New York state. Baldwin #3 was the former Monterey & Salinas Valley #1. Both engines had been used to construct the NC. The Utah Eastern sale included the first mention of an early caboose on the line. Research tends to indicate that it was the combination car acquired from the never-completed Stockton & Ione Railroad in 1879 and known on the NC as the "black caboose."

UP BUYS RAILROAD

On June 16, 1881 it was announced that the mighty Union Pacific Railway had purchased the little Nevada Central Railway, keeping the same name and officers, but adding an Executive Committee and three new directors from the UP: Charles Francis Adams, Sidney Dillon and Frederic Ames.

The UP purchase appears to have ended any further plans for building the proposed Nevada Southern and Nevada Northern lines as extensions of the Nevada Central.

The two new Baldwin Locomotive Works Class 8-20D 2-6-0s, already on order, arrived in 1881 and were soon named *S.H.H. Clark* (second #1) and *Sidney Dillon* (second #2). Clark was the UP's general superintendent and Dillon was its president. The new engines were painted olive green and gold with brass fixtures. They were equipped with diamond stacks and designed to burn coal.

The rather odd and sudden acquisition by the Union Pacific is interesting in that the big road had no physical connection with the narrow gauge. In fact, the nearest UP line was hundreds of miles away.

At this time General William Jackson Palmer was pushing his three-foot-gauge Denver & Rio Grande westward into Utah. The UP was fearful that the Rio Grande would build across central Nevada, connecting with the Nevada Central Railway and thus giving the D&RG a connection with the Central Pacific. The UP felt that this arrangement would be "prejudicial to its best interest." However, the NC was never integrated into the UP system.

BENEFITS NARROW GAUGE

Despite spending $959,500 to purchase the Nevada Central's capital stock and $250,000 for the outstanding bonds, the purchase proved to be a poor investment for the UP. It was a real benefit for the narrow gauge.

After acquiring the NC, the UP built a group of 20 new flat cars for the narrow gauge at its Omaha shops in 1881. Some of these cars were later rebuilt into stock, coal and box cars. Many were still around at the end of operations.

In December 1881, carmen at Battle Mountain completed what the *Battle Mountain Messenger* said was, "The finest passenger coach we have seen in many a day. The *Silver State* will be placed on the NC track in about a week." The red plush car seats with gold (bright brass) armrests, stove, wash stand and other accommodations where shipped

from Omaha. The car was painted buff, a color "that will not be affected by the alkali dust."

Soon after the Union Pacific's takeover, business over the desert and mountain narrow gauge began to decline. By 1882, much of the mining equipment and supplies for the southern camps began to flow over the Carson & Colorado's shorter route.

On December 22, 1882 the NC's Mason Bogie #2 was shipped to Ogden for use on the Utah & Northern Railway. This little 0-4-4 was the former American Fork *Onward*. The NC acquired it from the Eureka & Palisade in 1879. Officially named *Austin* on the NC, it was known simply as the "Dinky." The UP Omaha shops rebuilt the engine as an 0-4-2T in January 1883. It became U&N #45 and #296 in the 1885 UP system general renumbering. A small switcher, known as the "Dinky," was reportedly in service as Denver, South Park & Pacific #75 at Buena Vista, Colorado in the early 1880s. This could be the same rebuilt Bogie. UP records show her scrapped by 1887.

Operations on the NC improved under UP ownership, although profits did not. C. W. Hinchcliffe was retained to run the railroad, however, by January 1885 the UP allowed the NC to go into receivership.

Locals were up in arms when the narrow gauge hired Chinamen as firemen in a cost-cutting move. An 1886 Pacific traveler aboard a Central Pacific train at Battle Mountain noted that the fireman of the NC passenger train about to depart for Austin "was a Chinaman." Much discussion among the fellow passengers followed, but it was noted that the oriental seemed most capable.

The UP stated that the NC's stocks and bonds had little if any value. On June 21, 1888 the Nevada Central, under foreclosure, was turned back to the original bondholders, headed by Anson Stokes. The UP was happy to finally be relieved of what it said "has heretofore proved a heavy financial burden."

This view of NC's (second) #2 is the earliest known photograph of the Baldwin 2-6-0, built in 1881. She wears its original gold-leaf lettering with pinstriping and has both a crosshead pump and an injector. Number 2 was named the *Sidney Dillon* after the Union Pacific took control in June 1881. Author's collection

Nevada Central's #5 is pictured (above) in another J.H. Crockwell glass plate exposure made on the same day in early 1880 (see pages 38-39). In the consist are Carter Brother's box car #215 and former Monterey & Salinas Valley nine-window combine. The Central Pacific's passenger train has departed. Note the depot sign for D.W. Earl who served as forwarding agent for freight shipments. Author's collection

FORWARDING AND COMMISSION HOUSE,

228 CLAY STREET, SAN FRANCISCO,
109 AND 111 FRONT STREET, SACRAMENTO.

Railroad Depots : { RENO, WADSWORTH,
BATTLE MOUNTAIN, AND ELKO.

Battle Mountain September 1 1871.

M Dinsmore & Bros

To **D. W. EARL**, Dr.

Back Charges (_____ bills annexed) - - - - - - $ _____
Railroad Charges on 137 packages, 9578 pounds, $ 169,75
                                                $ _____
Forwarding - - - - - - - - - - - - - - - - $ 9,50 $179,25

Received Payment,

[JEFFERIS, Printer, Sac.]

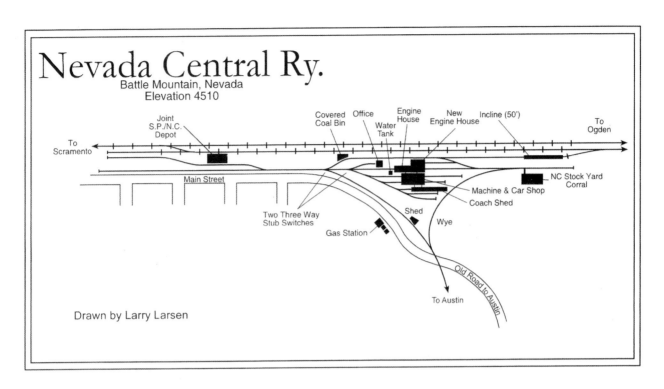

Nevada Central Ry.
Battle Mountain, Nevada
Elevation 4510

Drawn by Larry Larsen

BATTLE MOUNTAIN SHOPS

The Battle Mountain shops served the NC throughout its lifetime. They are depicted (above) in the mid-1930s and with employees (below) in 1887. The structures are (left to right) shop and office, enginehouse, water tank, machine and car shop. L.A. LeMaire-NENM

THE ONE SPOT

The Nevada Central's #1 (2nd) and sister (2nd) #2 came new from Baldwin in April 1881. Built as Baldwin's Class 8/20D-33 and 34, they had been ordered before the Union Pacific assumed control in June. After arrival, they were named *S.H.H. Clark* (#1) and *Sidney Dillon* (#2), for the UP's superintendent and president. The "One Spot" remained in service until 1923 and then supplied parts for #2. She waited out the years (below) at Battle Mountain in 1938. Richard B. Jackson

Both engines arrived with diamond stacks. Number One (right) is pictured with a capped straight stack in the late 1880s. Both locomotives later were converted back to diamond stacks. J.M. Hiskey collection

THE SILVER STATE

Pride of the Nevada Central was the ornate passenger coach *Silver State*. The car was built by James Bolan in the Battle Mountain car shop in 1881. The red plush, flowered seats with brass armrests came from Omaha. The *Battle Mountain Messenger* noted that it was "the finest passenger coach we have seen in many a day," adding that the car had a highly finished washstand and was one of the finest cars in the state. The buff painted coach was outshopped in December 1881 and was "somewhat scorched" a few days later due to a faulty stove pipe. Rarely used in later years, the car is now preserved at the California State Railroad Museum.

The 1937 interior view of the *Silver State* (top right) still shows the original flowered, red plush seats and fine woodwork. Richard B. Jackson

The car is draped in mourning (below) for a conductor who was murdered by a gambler a few days before. Automatic Janney couplers and air brakes date the photo to the post-1906 period when the car was reportedly painted steel gray with a brown letterboard. Author's collection

The *Silver State* was painted black with red trim and gold lettering in 1895. It is pictured with J.W. Twilliger (left) at Clifton. Linwood Moody Collection

Painted as the Central Pacific's *Stanford* (below), the *Silver State* took part in the Golden Gate International Exposition of 1939-40. Richard B. Jackson

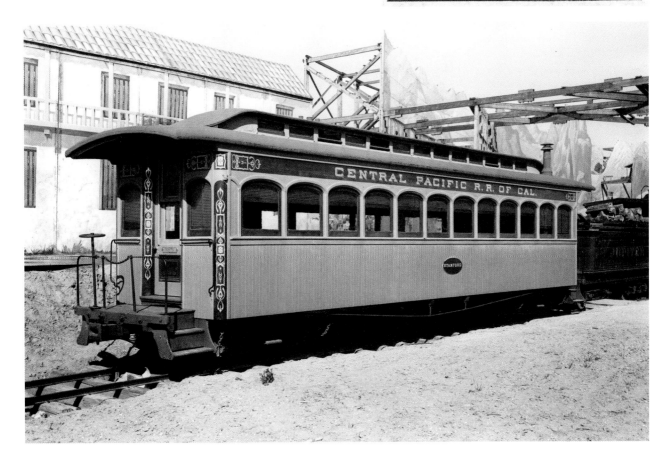

AUSTIN'S OWN... EMMA NEVADA

World famous opera star Emma Nevada was born at Alpha Diggins, California in 1859, but grew up in the rip-roaring mining town of Austin. Born Emma Wixom, her father was a doctor and her mother, a dealer in the local gambling hall, died when Emma was 13. Emma began singing at Austin's Methodist Church and later studied music and languages at Mills Seminary.

After graduation, she went to Europe in 1877 to study under Mme Marchesi in Vienna. Her voice brought her instant operatic success and she toured the continent. Emma even sang at the coronation of England's King George V. Her father soon joined her as manager.

In 1885 Emma Nevada began a triumphal tour of the United States. On December 4 she rode aboard the *Silver State* on a special Nevada Central train that was met in Clifton by Austin's leading citizens and the Lander Guard Band that struck up "Home Sweet Home." That evening she sang again for the entire town at the Methodist Church amid floral tributes and standing ovations.

Emma Nevada was married in Paris and was given a $100,000 diamond necklace by Queen Victoria. She died in Liverpool in 1940 at the age of 81, always telling of her childhood days in the Nevada mining town.

Emma Nevada, one of the 19th century's most famous opera stars, grew up in Austin and never forgot her roots. On her 1885 "Grand Tour" of America she drew huge crowds wherever she went. More than 2,000 cheered when she sang in Virginia City at Piper's Opera House. A NC special train took her back to Austin in 1885. Ward Kimball collection

When Emma Nevada came home to Austin aboard the *Silver State* in 1885, she was met at the station by a gaily decked carriage drawn by "all the young blades in town." That evening she sang again at the Methodist Church (right), where she began her singing career. Sketch by Paul Nyeland

When Ward Kimball rebuilt the NC's #2 (below), she was named *Emma Nevada*. Richard B. Jackson

Austin City Railway #1, the *Mules' Relief*, pauses at the joint ACRy/ NCRR freight office on Austin's Main Street in the mid-1880s. The flat car is loaded with cord wood for a mine or mill on Lander Hill, in the background. Wally Trapnell collection

Jonie Hill, ACM

CHAPTER 6
YOU GOTTA HAVE CONNECTIONS

The Austin City Ry | Battle Mountain & Lewis | Cortez Mines

 **AUSTIN CITY RAILWAY MULES' RELIEF**
When regular NC service began in March 1880, passengers and freight still did not reach downtown Austin, located high above and a mile or so away from the end of track at Clifton. Freighters charged high rates for the short haul into town and onto the mines and mills located on Lander Hill.

Allen A. Curtis, superintendent of the Manhattan Silver Mining Company, applied for a right-of-way for the Austin City Railway from the city fathers. The new line was planned to run from the Clifton depot up a 7.5% grade and down Austin's Main Street to the Manhattan Mill in upper Pony Canyon.

Curtis purchased the ties and iron rails from the NC on May 29, 1880, and construction on the line began two days later. Track laying reached the International Hotel in early August. This Virginia City hostelry had been taken down and moved piece by piece to Austin in 1863. It was re-erected on the corner of Main and Cedar.

Three-foot rails were soon extended to the Manhattan Mill and eventually to several mines on Lander Hill, giving the ACRy a total length of 2.8 miles.

51

STEEP CLIFTON GRADE

The grade out of Clifton was so steep that it was thought a steam locomotive would be unable to make the climb. So, for the first year, teams consisting of 11 mules were used to haul single-car trains up the hill.

A Nevada Central engineer thought otherwise and volunteered to see if his engine could make the grade. His 4-4-0 stormed up the hill and past the Citizen's Mill without difficulty. The demonstration convinced Superintendent Curtis, and he placed an order for a steam dummy 0-4-2T with the Baldwin Locomotive Works in late December of 1880.

The new dummy arrived in Battle Mountain on May 30, 1881. It was set up and tested by the NC's shop crew, and after some minor adjustments, ran down to Clifton. Named *Mules' Relief*, it had an ornate cab that fully enclosed the boiler. The engine was painted a light leather, with brown panels, gold striping and an olive drab tank. An iron pilot (cowcatcher) graced each end, and there were special attachments for brooms to keep the street rails clear of dirt.

The *Mules' Relief* was a popular design for street railways of the period because it was thought that the enclosed body would not panic horses and mules.

TEST LOCOMOTIVE

On the morning of June 17, 1881, a small crowd gathered at the top of the grade to see if the new locomotive would be able to make the climb up from Clifton. Allen Curtis invited a few friends to ride the engine with him and at 11:00 a.m. the *Mules' Relief* came smoking up to the foot of Main Street, whistle blowing and bell ringing. She was answered by mine and mill whistles on Lander Hill.

The next day the dummy pulled the second section of an excursion train to a picnic and baseball game at Waters. A small enginehouse was built of adobe blocks near the Manhattan Mill, and a joint NC/ACRy freight depot was constructed on a Main Street siding between the Lander County Court House and Nicholas' Lumber Yard.

Although there was room aboard the *Mules' Relief* for several passengers, there is no indication that regular passenger service was offered. The Nevada Central maintained a ticket office in the International Hotel, and it is likely that the Dummy Line did carry some passengers to and from Clifton.

In August 1882, workmen were extending and improving the ACRy tracks during the day, so the railway ran at night. On the night of August 19 Engineer Andy Wright began his trip down to Clifton from the Manhattan Mill. The steam brake was not working, but Wright thought he and Fireman Frank Duffy could ease the engine down the 7.5% grade using the handbrakes, against Allen Curtis' advice.

At about 6:00 a.m., while passing the *Reveille* newspaper office, the *Mules' Relief* began to pick up speed. Handbrakes and reversing the Johnson Bar were not enough to slow the runaway. The dummy locomotive left the tracks on a sharp curve above the Citizen's Mill, landing on its side 75 feet below the edge of a cliff.

The driving force behind the Austin City Railway was Allen A. Curtis (top), superintendent of the Manhattan Silver Mining Company. The mining company (below), owned mines on Lander Hill and a mill in upper Austin. Author's collection

The *Mules' Relief* was built by Baldwin in 1881 as a steam dummy. She is pictured near the joint ACRy/NCRR freight office with NC box car #209 (above) and at the three-way stub switch near the Clifton depot (below) in 1881. Author's collection

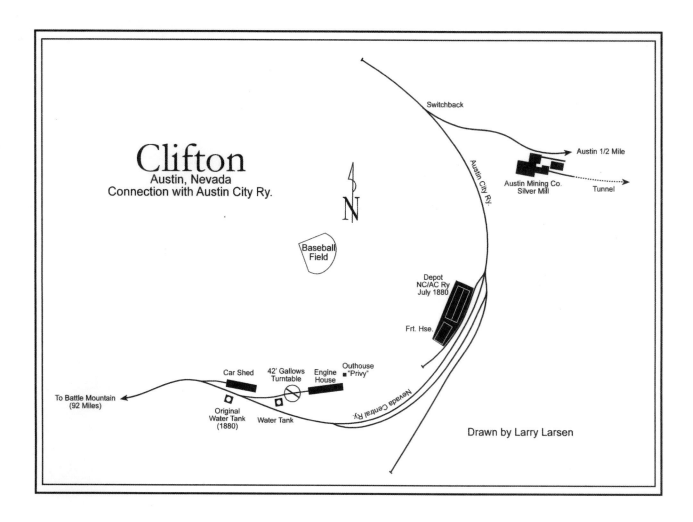

Clifton
Austin, Nevada
Connection with Austin City Ry.

N

Switchback

Austin 1/2 Mile

Austin Mining Co.
Silver Mill

Tunnel

Austin City Ry.

Baseball
Field

Depot
NC/AC Ry
July 1880

Frt. Hse.

Car Shed

42' Gallows
Turntable

Engine
House

Outhouse
"Privy"

Nevada Central Ry.

To Battle Mountain
(92 Miles)

Original
Water Tank
(1880)

Water Tank

Drawn by Larry Larsen

ENGINEER DIES

Engineer Wright was killed, while Fireman Duffy was able to jump clear. The *Mules' Relief* had its superstructure and clerestory roof demolished. It had been in service for only three months.

The battered engine was hauled back to the mill's machine shop and rebuilt along the lines of a typical saddletanker, with an oversize cab. J. F. Hill came over from Ruby Hill to run the rebuilt locomotive and Frank Duffy continued his fireman's duties. The *Mules' Relief* was now simply #1.

In 1884, trackage was extended to several other mines and dumps on Lander Hill by using switchbacks. However, by the late 1880s, both mining and milling decreased. The *Reese River Reveille* reported that on the evening of February 2, 1887, "A fire burned the Engine House and Motor that runs on the Austin City Railway." Exactly how much damage was done is not known.

The Manhattan Silver Mining Company's mines, mill and concentrator closed in 1889. Traffic over the ACRy all but came to an end. The *Battle Mountain Messenger* on June 29, 1893 said, "The Mules' Relief came down from Austin for repairs in the Nevada Central shops." There is no indication that she ever returned to Austin. That same year a flash flood, caused by a cloud burst, wiped out some of the ACRy tracks.

By the early 1970s one of the few reminders that there had ever been a railroad down the center of Austin's Main Street was the small enginehouse. The adobe structure began to crack and "melt," so it was torn down in 1974-75. Today, little remains of this NC feeder line. Portions of U.S. 50 are built on parts of the ACRy grade atop Lander Hill, down Pony Canyon and along Austin's historic Main Street.

Before the Austin City Railway was built from the Nevada Central's end of track at Clifton, supplies had to be hauled by 20 mule teams. Jerry Mock collection

The ACRy enginehouse (below) still stood in 1972. John E. Robinson

MULES' RELIEF

Following the runaway accident that killed Engineer Andy Wright early on the morning of August 20, 1882, the *Mules' Relief* was rebuilt without the fancy steam dummy cab. Author and Wally Trapnell collections

The *Mules' Relief* is pictured (above) switching cars at the Clifton depot in about 1886 and pausing with the crew (right) in 1888. Note that the NC's car house and freighthouse have not yet been built, and the water tank is at its original location.

Austin City Railway's *Mules' Relief* heads upgrade to Lander Hill (opposite, top) with a flat car load of cordwood in c. 1887. The site is the siding near 6th Street. Lander Hill mines and mill of the Manhattan Silver Mining Co. are shown (opposite, lower) along with the ACRy in an 1881 engraving. Both, author's collection

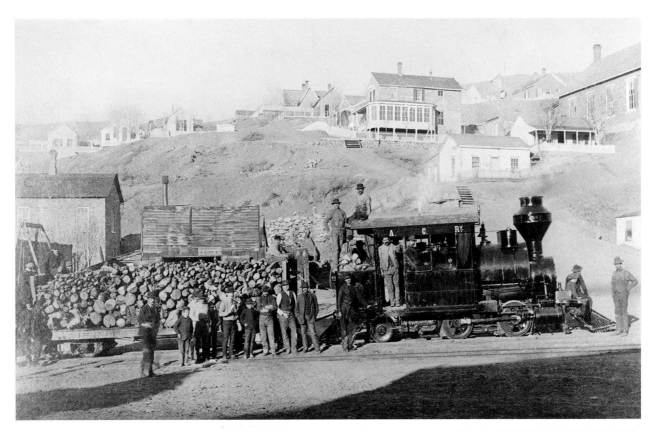

NO.1. LANDER SHAFT, -2. CURTIS SHAFT, -3. FROST SHAFT, -4. NORTH STAR SHAFT, -5. OREGON SHAFT, -6. RUBY INCLINE, -7. PACIFIC SHAFT, -8. SAVANNAH SHAFT,
NO.9. FLORIDA INCLINE,   NO.11. MILL BUILDINGS,
NO.10. MAGNOLIA INCLINE,   MANHATTAN SILVER MINING COMPANY,   NO.12. CONCENTRATOR.
                                   AUSTIN, LANDER CO. NEVADA

The 0-4-2T pauses on the Main Street siding, near the
courthouse in c. 1887. Pictured left to right are Frank Dixon,
George Alsopp, Frank Merrigan, Engineer J.F. Hill and young
George McIntire. Linwood Moody collection

MAKING THE GRADE

The rebuilt *Mules' Relief* climbs the 7.5% grade out of Clifton
in 1885 (right) near the Citizen's Custom Silver Mill, site of
the 1882 runaway that killed the engineer. Nevada Historical
Society

The *Mules' Relief* heads up Main Street and past the International Hotel with a short train in the 1880s. Jerry Mock collection

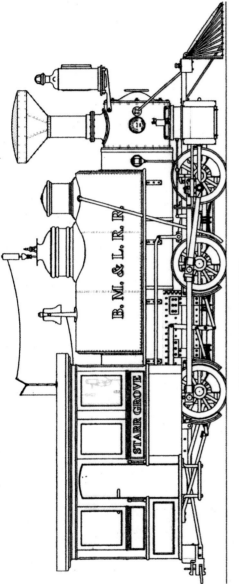

RIGHT SIDE VIEW

BATTLE MOUNTAIN & LEWIS R.R.

ENGINE NO. 2 AS IT PROBABLY LOOKED
UPON COMPLETION IN 1881

Drawn by Robert D. Bailey

SCALE   0 1 2 3 4 5 6

BUILT AT THE UNION IRON WORKS, SAN FRANCISCO, CA.

THIS DRAWING DEVELOPED FROM P S & C DRAWING NO. 1464.
DETAILS COPIED FROM SIMILAR P S & C LOCOMOTIVES.

PRESCOTT, SCOTT & CO.
SAN FRANCISCO
No. 27
1881
BUILDERS

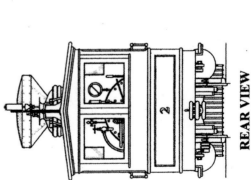

FRONT VIEW

REAR VIEW

BATTLE MOUNTAIN & LEWIS RAILROAD

Shortly after completion of the Nevada Central, gold assaying at $3,000 per ton was discovered in Lewis Canyon, 10 miles east of the new narrow gauge. The Starr Grove Mining Company formed the Battle Mountain & Lewis Railroad to connect the new camp and mines at Lewis.

Grading for the BM&L began on January 28, 1881 from the Nevada Central, 10.9 miles south of Battle Mountain. The location, originally known as Galena, was renamed Lewis Junction. Construction went rapidly across the generally level desert, with only one curve before reaching Lewis' lower town. Grading was completed by April 25. Under Construction Foreman Tom Rice, track layers reached Lewis Station on July, 30, 1881. A grand ball was held at Lower Town that evening.

Initial operations over the Lewis Line were made in June with the Nevada Central's #4, the *D. B. Hatch*, a former Monterey & Salinas Valley 4-4-0. On August 12 the BM&L received its new 2-4-0T *John D. Hall*, named for the road's president. Built by the Union Iron Works (Prescott, Scott & Company) of San Francisco, the little engine weighed 17 tons and cost $7,500. A small enginehouse was built at Lewis Station.

BM&L Superintendent Linn Bradberry Ball had the new engine take an excursion from Lewis Station to Battle Mountain, where a gala dance was held. The 2-4-0T had little trouble handling its train across the flat sagebrush country.

FOUR SWITCHBACKS

Tracks were then extended up Lewis Canyon during the latter half of 1881. The steep, twisting grade reached the Highland Chief, Starr Grove and Eagle mines, utilizing four switchbacks. The total length of the BM&L was 11.5 miles.

At Lewis Station the Starr Grove Mill was already in operation when the Eagle Mine's 15-stamp mill was built. With new mining activity, Lewis Station (called Lower Town) quickly grew to a reported 700 souls by the end of 1881. In 1881-82 the Highland Chief constructed its own 40-stamp mill.

It was soon apparent that the little *John D. Hall* was incapable of pulling itself, much less a train, up the canyon grade which reached 7.5% on the upper 2 1/2 miles. An agreement was made with the Union Iron Works to return the engine and replace it with a new, more powerful 0-6-0T named *Starr Grove*.

In the meantime, the BM&L again rented a Nevada Central locomotive. NC's Baldwin #5, the *Gen'l J. H. Ledlie* was able to handle the grades despite her 4-4-0 wheel arrangement. A double brake on its tender helped when coming down the switchbacks from the mines. Tom War-

ren served as BM&L's conductor on these runs, while "Web" Webster was the line's engineer.

The performance of the former North Pacific Coast engine on the BM&L was noted in the September 22, 1881 *Railway Age*, which stated the engine "is now running on a branch with 395 feet grade to the mile, hauling 2 cars of freight."

MINE CLOSES

In February 1882, Starr Grove's Superintendent Bothwell cut miners pay, and the mine shut down when the men refused to work. An attempt to reopen the mine resulted in three shootings, and the miner's union from Austin chartered a special train to bring some 250 armed men to Lewis, in order to support the striking men. Before the train arrived, the Starr Grove Mine reinstated the wage cuts, and the miners returned to work. When the miner's union special returned to Austin, a victory celebration parade, complete with brass band, marched down Main Street.

In March 1882, the Starr Grove Mill made a $20,000 bullion shipment, but their railroad was in trouble. The Nevada Central attached the little railroad for $522 in back rent on the *General Ledlie*, $4,898 in unpaid freight charges and an additional $1,017 for coal. The BM&L could not pay the debt and shut down, sending a wagon to Lewis Junction for passengers and express shipments bound for the gold camp.

The Starr Grove Mining Company was also insolvent and was sold by the Lander County sheriff in April 1882. Lewis mining man H. D. Gates bought the BM&L for $4,401. Spring washouts in Lewis Canyon were being repaired the next month when the Eagle Mine and Mill also suspended operations. With few prospects for a revival of BM&L operations, Superintendent Ball quit, and by mid-June the Lewis Railroad was all but finished.

And what about the line's second locomotive *Starr Grove*? Union Iron Works never delivered it to the BM&L. The engine was later sold to the Central American & Pacific Railway & Transportation Company in Guatemala.

MINE EXPLOSION

A boiler explosion occurred in the Betty O'Neal Mine's 260-foot shaft, west of Lower Town on October 31, 1882. Repairs to the mine saw the Nevada Central operating several trains over BM&L rails. However, a fire at the Betty O'Neal resulted in the workings being closed for good.

Several more trains ventured over the BM&L in 1883 when machinery from the Starr Grove Mill was removed and taken over the NC to Ledlie, where mule teams hauled it to Bernice, a mining camp 60 miles away. Occasional trains were operated over the BM&L by NC crews in March 1885, but the short revival in gold mining was soon ended by another miner's strike.

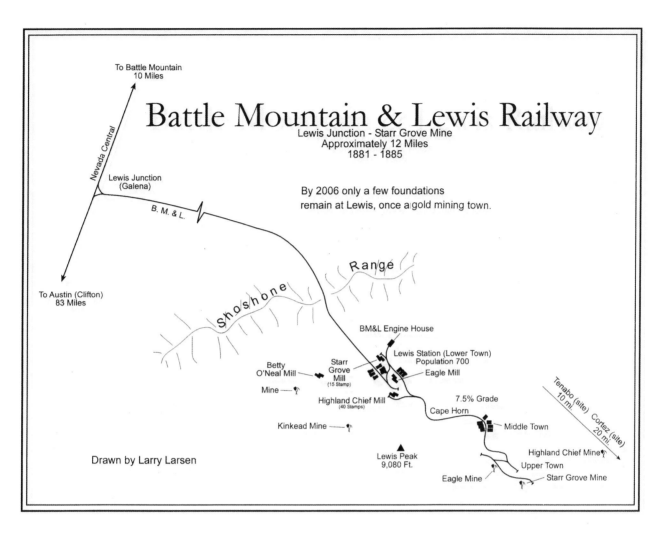

Battle Mountain & Lewis Railway
Lewis Junction - Starr Grove Mine
Approximately 12 Miles
1881 - 1885

To Battle Mountain
10 Miles

Nevada Central

Lewis Junction
(Galena)

B. M. & L.

To Austin (Clifton)
83 Miles

By 2006 only a few foundations
remain at Lewis, once a gold mining town.

Shoshone Range

BM&L Engine House

Lewis Station (Lower Town)
Population 700

Betty
O'Neal Mill

Starr
Grove
Mill
(15 Stamp)

Eagle Mill

Mine

Highland Chief Mill
(40 Stamps)

7.5% Grade

Cape Horn

Tenabo (site) 10 mi.
Cortez (site) 20 mi.

Kinkead Mine

Middle Town

Highland Chief Mine

Upper Town

Lewis Peak
9,080 Ft.

Eagle Mine

Starr Grove Mine

Drawn by Larry Larsen

The BM&L was sold for back taxes to J. A. Blossom in October 1887. He planned to relocate the entire railroad in Crum Canyon, near Pittsburg, Nevada, the scene of another brief-lived mining boom. The final end of the BM&L came in 1890, when its rails were removed.

Paul P. Thompson collection

CORTEZ MINES, LTD. RAILROAD

Cortez, a 30" gauge Porter 0-4-0T, charges upgrade enroute to the mine on Tenabo Mountain. The train snakes around a sharp curve (above) with four small, four-wheel ore cars in the early 1890s. The author found the little engine on display at Las Vegas (opposite top) in 1954. Cortez was once a wild and wooly mining camp with frequent shootings. "Big Bill" Broadwater killed John Liewelyn (opposite lower) in a card game. He escaped the two guards taking him to Austin for trial and was later captured in California. "Big Bill" was sentenced to 20 years in the Carson City prison.
Sketch by Paul Nyeland

CORTEZ MINES LTD. RAILROAD

The isolated Cortez silver mine was located some 24 miles southeast of Battle Mountain. The mill and small settlement of Cortez (pronounced Cor-dits) was about a mile from the mine, located up a steep ravine on the side of Tenabo Mountain.

Although the area was served by the three-foot-gauge lines of the Nevada Central RR and the brief-lived Battle Mountain & Lewis Ry., the 30" gauge Cortez Mines Limited Railroad did not connect with any other road. Just over the mountain range to the east ran the Eureka & Palisade.

Silver discoveries had been made in the area in the early 1860s, but Indian troubles and the Civil War had kept the mines from being worked until the late 1880s. The camp was a typical wild and wooly frontier mining town with frequent gun fights and its share of bad men. The Cortez Mines, Ltd. built a stamp mill and a short, steep, twisting 30" gauge railroad between the mine and mill in 1890.

CORTEZ TO BEOWAWE

Outshopped by H. K. Porter & Company, the eight-ton 0-4-0T *Cortez* (c/n 1196, July 1890) was consigned to Beowawe on the Central Pacific. Wagons hauled the #1 to the mill. Likewise, a half-dozen wooden side-dump ore cars and a flat car came from a Denver mining supply company. It is interesting to note that the mining company reasoned that their equipment should be constructed to a gauge of 29 3/4" in order to fit the 30" gauge track.

Silver mining at Cortez ceased during WWI, and the little 0-4-0T was tucked away in the small enginehouse and forgotten. The small wooden ore cars were left scattered about.

In the late 1940s, the *Cortez* and its cars were discovered by Robert Caudill, better known as Dobie Doc. Caudill was a real Western character who went about rescuing everything from stagecoaches to cable cars.

Dobie displayed some of his "finds" at the Last Frontier Hotel on the Las Vegas strip, which was once part of his cattle ranch. His collection included a narrow gauge Shay from the Pioche Pacific, a former Florence & Cripple Creek 2-8-0, the *Cortez* and cars from the Nevada Central and Eureka & Palisade.

Some confusion arose when Caudill lettered the 0-4-0T for the Ruby Hill R.R., a three-foot-gauge mining road at Eureka, Nevada. The *Cortez* engine and several cars were later displayed at various sites in the Las Vegas-Boulder City area. It is now owned by three California railfans.

CORTEZ MINES

Nevada collector "Dobie Doc" found the 1890 Porter in a small shed at Cortez and displayed it and several cars at his Last Frontier Museum in Las Vegas. He had the engine lettered for the *Ruby Hill RR* (above), a 36" gauge mining line at Eureka. The author found it there (above) in 1954. By 1961, the incorrect lettering had been painted over (opposite top). The small flat car (opposite right) had radial coupler pockets in order to negotiate sharp curves. Several Cortez mines ore cars were found abandoned in a canyon (opposite left) in 1986. Author's photographs

An excursion train passes through the Reese River Canyon (below) in 1887. Baldwin Mogul #2 (2nd) sports a tall capped smokestack added during the period the Nevada Central was controlled by the Union Pacific. In the consist are a boxcar and two combines. Passengers have climbed the rocky outcropping (opposite page) in both views. Barbara Powell, NCNM

CHAPTER 7

93 MILES OF SAGEBRUSH

 DURING THE PERIOD of Union Pacific control (1881-1888), the NC's equipment and operations improved, although the traffic declined. C. W. Hinchliffe was retained by Omaha as the NC's general manager. He was able to keep the road in good condition and improve efficiency, despite a decline in mining revenues.

The box and flat car fleets were painted yellow by late 1881. Passenger equipment was repainted "buff and nicely varnished." This pale yellow color was selected, again, because it would not be effected by alkali dust kicked up by passing trains.

New Baldwin Mogul #1 (2nd) was rebuilt with an extended smokebox and straight-capped stack in an effort to improve steaming and reduce coal consumption. Coal cost $12 per ton delivered at Battle Mountain. The conversion was deemed successful and 2-6-0 #2 (2nd) received the same modifications in September 1886. Both engines retained their crosshead pump (engineer's side) and Sellers #5 injector (fireman's side) with which they were built.

Oddly enough 1876-built 4-4-0 #5, which had always been a good steaming engine, never received an extended smokebox and kept its diamond stack and pair of injectors. It did receive brakes on all tender trucks as it was used occasionally on the steep 7.5% Battle Mountain and Lewis grades.

UP DEFAULTS

In January 1885 the Union Pacific defaulted on the NC's bonds. The UP considered its $959,500 investment in the NC to be "virtually worthless." General Manager Hinchcliffe was named as Receiver, and on June 21, 1887, the NC was returned to the original bondholders. The now independent NC was again under the control of the Anson Phelps Stokes interests. D. B. Hatch was named president, C. W. Henchcliffe stayed on as general superintendent and secretary, while Stokes himself was treasurer.

Famed Comstock photographer James H. Crockwell visited the NC in June 1887. His views of a picnic train pulled by cap-stacked #2 provide the best documentation of changes to equipment under the five years of UP control. The "Two Spot" now sported the extended smokebox and a new steam brake that was applied in September 1886. The combination cars were buff-colored, while a lone boxcar was painted yellow.

The 1890s saw a further decline in mining but annual increases in cattle shipments by local ranchers. The Manhattan Silver Mine and Mill, long the biggest shipper over the NC and its main reason for being built, shut down in 1890. During this period, a typical train consisted of only a locomotive and single combine. Hard times had befallen the NC. Except for a few passengers and the U.S. mail, regular trains would not have run at all. Of course there were the usual engine breakdowns, delays and derailments associated with lack of traffic, loss of revenue and reduced maintenance.

In 1890-91 Anson Stokes' Austin Mining Company began drilling a 6,000-foot-long exploration tunnel from near the Nevada Central's terminal at Clifton. Known as the Austin-Manhattan drainage and hauling tunnel, it was intended to tap the lower levels of Lander Hill. A new 40-stamp mill was built at Clifton, but production never justified its cost.

STRUGGLES ALONG

For the next 50 years the Nevada Central struggled along against seemingly impossible odds with aging equipment and further reductions in area mining activity. Each winter saw temperatures of 38 below zero, often accompanied by snowdrifts that packed canyon cuts and blocked the line for days at a time.

Following an early January 1890 blizzard, the first train did not get through to Austin until the 23rd. The storm also affected the Central Pacific as the Battle Mountain

paper noted that the railroad's cyclone (rotary) snowplow had passed through. The NC was again blocked in February, and #2 was badly wrecked while trying to clear the line. It was rebuilt by Master Mechanic W. E. Killen with a pair of injectors replacing the crosshead-activated pump.

Boilermaker James Perkins built an iron-faced wedge snowplow in 1891, using an existing flat car. The following year, Perkins constructed a steam-driven pile driver on the deck of another flat.

Spring often saw the normally placid Reese River raging out of its banks, washing out trestles and trackage. July could bring temperatures in excess of 100 degrees, accompanied by sunkinks that derailed trains.

Fall was a time for increasingly important stock shipments with extra crews and doubleheaded trains. In order to handle the livestock movements, several flat cars were rebuilt as open-top stock cars in 1894. These cattle cars were crude affairs built in the Battle Mountain shop by J. C. Slater. Four more "new" stock cars were turned out the next year, with a corresponding decrease in flat cars.

LINE SHOWS LOSS

By 1895, the three passenger cars (combines #1, #2 and *Silver State*) were painted dark brown. Freight equipment was repainted boxcar red during this period, replacing the earlier yellow paint.

Despite all the efforts to drum up business, the line showed a net loss of $244.47 for 1896. The following year, J. F. Mitchell was named general manager. Mitchell lasted only two months, before his assistant, Frank E. Jones, assumed the general manager position.

Battle Mountain shopmen completed another rebuild of 2-6-0 #1 in 1895. Master Mechanic J. C. Slater added a further extension to the smokebox which contained metal screens in order to reduce the chance of sparks, improve steaming and reduce coal consumption. Upon completion, the freshly-painted One Spot was photographed with shopmen and other employees. Recently outshopped former Monterey & Salinas Valley combination car #1 was coupled up with #1 for several more photos.

The train schedule was varied in order to connect with the Central Pacific (Southern Pacific) trains at Battle Mountain. A typical timetable (1896) called for an 8:15 a.m. southbound departure, arriving in Austin at 2:00 p.m. (Tuesday, Thursday, Saturday). Northbound trains left Austin at 7:00 a.m., arriving in Battle Mountain at 12:55 p.m. (Monday, Wednesday, Friday). As with many short lines, the NC did not run on Sunday.

In 1897, Anson Phelps Stokes sent his son J. G. Phelps Stokes to Nevada to oversee his mining and railroad properties. Young Stokes was a recent graduate of Yale's Sheffield Scientific School and also had a medical degree from Columbia University.

CASTLE BUILT ON HILL

The "Stokes Castle" was built as a residence for the younger Stokes. Constructed of native stone, the tower was built on a hill west of Austin. The ground floor contained a kitchen and dining room, with the living room and bath on the second floor. Two bedrooms occupied the top floor, and balconies provided fresh air and an excellent view. Although the castle was only occupied for a few years, the younger Stokes would stay involved with the Nevada Central for four decades.

That fall the local newspaper reported "a brisk freight and cattle business." However, it was always feast or famine, with the latter more often being the case.

More flats were converted to carry livestock in June of 1898, just in time for a large cattle shipment of 1,000 head during the first week of July. Eventually the roster showed 14 of these homemade cars, which retained their old flat car numbers.

An assessment of $120 per $1,000 Nevada Central bond was made in 1898. Of the $750,000 total bonds issued, 33 bondholders failed to pay the assessment. The Nevada Company of New Jersey was formed to guarantee the semiannual interests on the remaining $717,000 bonds, beginning on July 1, 1898. Anson Stokes' other mining and milling properties were also part of the holding company.

In 1900, J. G. Phelps Stokes offered the Nevada Central to Collis P. Huntington as part of a short cut route to Southern California. Huntington, last of the transcontinental route's "Big Four" politely replied "...the material in your little road is so light that it would hardly be of any use to us..." The NC would have to go it alone. A new century and a few changes were in the narrow gauge's future.

In 1897 Anson Phelps Stokes sent his son J.G. Phelps Stokes to Nevada to oversee his mining and railroad interests. The "Stokes Castle" (right) was built near Austin as younger Stokes' living quarters. The stone castle remains today as a local landmark. John P. Killoran

The 1885 Nevada Central pass (opposite page) is from the author's collection.

PICNIC TRAIN

NC's picnic train on June 2, 1887 was without a doubt the most photographed train of the 1880s. The #2 is shown in a rocky canyon with yellow painted boxcar and combines #1 and #2. Engine #2 has an extended smokebox and tall capped stack.
CSRM

Excursionists decorate the pilot beam of Mogul 2 as they pose for famed Western photographer James H. Crockwell at Ledlie on June 2, 1887. Both combines #1 and #2 were rebuilt from nine windows on each side to seven windows in August 1886. *Wally Trapnell collection*

EXCURSION TRAIN

The excursion of June 2, 1887 reached the picnic site in the hill country north of Austin where tents were erected. Mogul #2 provides the background for these James H. Crockwell photographs. Note the extended smokebox and straight stack, which has replaced the earlier diamond stack. Wally Trapnell collection

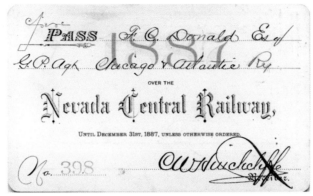

This 1887 annual pass is from the author's collection.

The Nevada Central's general offices and downtown ticket office occupied a stone building at 63 Main Street in Austin. Stokes' other interests here included the State Bank of Nevada, the Nevada Company and Austin Mining Company. Nevada Historical Society

This 1890 annual pass is from the author's collection.

Mogul #1 (2nd) has just undergone a rebuilding (below) in c. 1895. The smokebox has received a further extension in an attempt to improve steaming and reduce coal consumption. The crosshead pump has been removed and the boiler jacket patched. L.A. Lemaire, Guy Dunscomb collection

The NEVADA CENTRAL R. R. CO.

ROUND TRIP TICKET.
GOOD FOR ONE FIRST CLASS PASSAGE

Form 44

2340

Battle Mtn

— TO —

Austin

When Officially Stamped or Signed by the Agent.

SUBJECT TO THE FOLLOWING CONTRACT.

IN CONSIDERATION of this Ticket being sold at a rate less than the regular full first class rate, the purchaser hereby agrees that it will not be good for passage after **THIRTY (30) DAYS** after the date of sale as stamped on the back hereof: also, that this Ticket is **NOT TRANSFERABLE** and shall be **VOID** if not presented and fully used for passage before midnight of its date of expiration, and that he failing to comply with this agreement. Conductors may refuse to accept this Ticket and demand the full regular fare which he agrees to pay.

Baggage checked to destination only.
Limit of baggage liability One Hundred Dollars.
IN NO CASE WILL THE LIMIT OF THIS TICKET BE EXTENDED.

☞ **NOTICE to Passenger:**—In case of error on part of Agent, or question of doubt between holder and conductor, pay the latter's claim, take his receipt, and all errors or irregularities reported to the General Office will be promptly and satisfactorily adjusted.

I hereby agree to all the provisions of the above contract:

John P. Carroll

Ticket must be signed by purchaser.

GOOD AS NEW

Battle Mountain shop men pose with recently-outshopped combine #1 and Mogul #1 (below) in c. 1895. The changes were apparently not successful, and by 1900 the engine was converted back to a short smokebox and diamond stack. The combination car was painted dark brown during this period. J.M. Hiskey collection from G.M. Best, coach lamp sketch by Jim Scancarelli

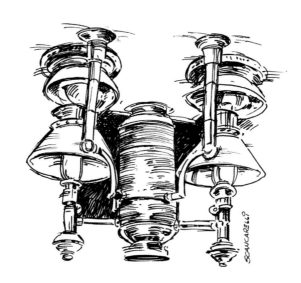

THE NEVADA CENTRAL RAILROAD COMPANY.

No 11 TIME TABLE No 11

TO TAKE EFFECT SUNDAY, NOVEMBER 12, 1899, AT 6 O'CLOCK, A. M.

For the Information and Government of Employees Only. The Right to Vary this Time Table or These Rules is Reserved.

TRAINS GOING SOUTH			Length of Siding in No. of Cars	Distance from Austin.	STATIONS and SIDINGS.	Distance from Battle Mountain	Telegraph Calls	Station Nos.	TRAINS GOING NORTH		
		No. 1. ACCOMMODATION, Leaving TUESDAY, THURSDAY, SATURDAY.							No. 2. ACCOMMODATION, Leaving MONDAY, WEDNESDAY, FRIDAY.		
		Depart							Arrive.		
....	....	7.30 A.M.	300	93	**BATTLE MOUNTAIN†**	......	BM S	1	1.30 P.M	....	....
					$10\frac{1}{2}$						
....	....	8.07 "	12	$82\frac{1}{2}$	LEWIS JUNCTION	$10\frac{1}{2}$		11	12.54 "	....	....
					$3\frac{1}{2}$						
....	....	8.20 "	......	79	DILLON †	14	DN	14	12.42 "	....	....
					$4\frac{3}{4}$						
....	....	8.35 "	3	$74\frac{1}{4}$	*BAILEYS	$18\frac{3}{4}$	......	19	12.25 "	....	....
					$16\frac{1}{4}$						
....	....	9.30 "	10	$57\frac{1}{2}$	WATTS†	$35\frac{1}{2}$	H	35	11.32 A.M.	....	....
					8						
....	....	9.57 "	6	$49\frac{1}{2}$	BRIDGES	$43\frac{1}{2}$	B	43	11.05 "	....	....
					10						
....	....	10 35 "	16	$39\frac{2}{3}$	*CANYON	$53\frac{1}{3}$	......	54	10.25 "	....	....
					3						
....	....	10.46 "	......	$36\frac{2}{3}$	WALTERS †	$56\frac{1}{3}$	W	56	10.15 "	....	....
					$3\frac{2}{3}$						
....	....	11.00 "	......	33	*RAVENSWOOD	60	......	60	10.03 "	....	....
					$2\frac{4}{5}$						
....	....	11.11 "	13	30	*VAUGHN'S	$62\frac{4}{5}$	......	62	9.53 "	....	....
					$6\frac{1}{2}$						
....	....	11.35 "	40	$23\frac{2}{3}$	*CURTIS	$69\frac{1}{3}$	......	69	9.29 "	....	....
					1						
....	....	11.40 "	40	$22\frac{3}{4}$	SILVER CREEK†	$70\frac{1}{4}$	SC	70	9.25 "	....	....
					$4\frac{1}{4}$						
....	....	11.55 "	20	$18\frac{7}{8}$	*CATON'S	$74\frac{1}{2}$	......	74	9.10 "	....	....
					$11\frac{5}{8}$						
....	....	12.40 P.M.	30	$6\frac{7}{8}$	AUSTIN JUNCTION†	$86\frac{1}{8}$	D	86	8.30 "	....	....
					$6\frac{7}{8}$						
....	....	1.10 P.M	40	......	**AUSTIN†**	93	Z Mc	93	8.00 A.M.	....	....
		Arrive.							Depart.		

☞ * Flag Stations. † Water Stations.

Trains must not exceed Twenty miles per hour under any circumstances. Read Rules on back of Card Carefully. Note Changes.

Conductors must see that they are supplied with Lamps, Flags, Tools, etc., and be on hand with Train ready to leave, and all freight and baggage loaded, Thirty Minutes before leaving time.

All trains will register at AUSTIN and BATTLE MOUNTAIN. IN CASE OF DOUBT, ALWAYS TAKE THE SAFE SIDE.

J. G. PHELPS STOKES,
PRESIDENT.

A. C. LUCK,
GENERAL MANAGER.

CHAS. L. McFAUL, ASSISTANT GENERAL MANAGER.

23 BROAD STREET, NEW YORK, June 2,1900.

Mr. J. G. Phelps Stokes,

    President, Nevada Central R. R. Co.

        47 Cedar St., New York.

My dear Sir:-

      Your letter of the 29th of May has come to hand, and in reply I would say that I will be glad to see you at almost any time when convenient to yourself.   As a matter of fact, it is somewhat doubtful if we shall build through the Reese River Valley, and if we do, the material in your little road is so light that it would hardly be of any use to us for the heavier road. This, however, is a matter we can talk about when I see you. Meantime I remain

        Yours very truly,

        C P Huntington

NC's #1 leaves Battle Mountain with a mixed train, trailed by combine #2 and the *Silver State* in about 1907. The engine now has a short smokebox and diamond stack. All three passenger accommodations appear in this rare action photograph. The combines were lettered for Wells Fargo & Company at this time. The open top stock cars still use link and pin couplers, while other cars have Janney automatic couplers. J.M. Hiskey, Linwood Moody collection

The Wells Fargo pass (opposite) is from the author's collection.

CHAPTER 8

HARD TIMES FOR THE SLIM GAUGE

 THE DAWN OF A NEW CENTURY did not bring a resurgence in the mining traffic that had both fostered and sustained the NC in earlier years. There were sporadic gold, silver and copper discoveries from time to time, although they were generally small, brief-lived strikes that added little to the NC's bottom line. Seasonal livestock shipments and the U.S. Mails kept the road alive.

Operations on the narrow gauge continued a slow decline that had begun with the closing of the Manhattan Silver Mining Company's mines and mill in 1890. The two connecting slim gauge carriers had also been abandoned. Battle Mountain & Lewis rails were removed in 1890, and the little Mules' Relief Line shut down in 1893.

Gold was discovered in southern Nevada in May 1900, and the Tonopah Gold Rush was attracting thousands to the desert country. The NC ran a preliminary survey to the new diggings, using portions of the Nevada Southern's planned route of the early 1880s. There was also talk of the NC being converted to standard gauge as part of Simon Bamberger's proposed Nevada Midland Railroad, but by October of 1902 this plan was dead, and nothing further was accomplished on an extension of the NC.

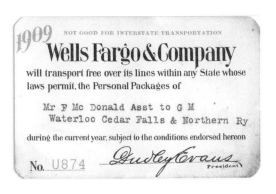

C&C RAILROAD HITS BONANZA

The Carson & Colorado Railway's three-foot-gauge tracks were much closer to the new bonanza. The C&C had been purchased by Southern Pacific in March 1900, two months prior to Jim Butler's Tonopah discovery. The SP was said to have recovered the $2,750,000 it paid Darius Ogden Mills for the C&C within two years. Again, the C&C had proven a better route to the "Southern Mines."

John Merr Hiskey hired out as the Nevada Central's auditor in 1901. He would remain with the road for the next 38 years and become the main reason it lasted as long as it did. J. G. Phelps Stokes was now content to oversee operations from his Cedar Street office in New York City. The Stokes Castle stood unused as a sentinel on the hill above Austin.

same manner. American Standard #5 never received the earlier modifications and retained her short smokebox and diamond stack.

In February 1901, a sudden thawing of some 20" of winter snows and a cloudburst near Vaughns brought flooding that washed out much of the trackage between Twenty Seven Mile Hill (near Helena) and Bridges (Milepost 43). A number of bridges suffered damage, and the two major ones in the Reese River Canyon were washed out. All hands joined in to repair the damage, and trains were running again in a week. The same winter thaw and thunderstorms also did great damage to the Southern Pacific and nearby Eureka & Palisade. Yearly floods would be a problem for the NC and E&P throughout their lifetimes.

Cloudbursts caused frequent washouts on the NC. Shop Foreman J.W. Treat surveys Reese River Canyon flood damage in 1910.
NENM

By 1901 the Nevada Central was running only three trains a week. In May, Mogul #2 emerged from a lengthy rebuild in the Battle Mountain shop sporting a short smokebox and diamond stack. The "Two Spot" looked very much as it had when built new by Baldwin 20 years earlier. Apparently the extended smokeboxes, with internal screens and capped straight stacks applied during the Union Pacific years, had proved to be less efficient and more maintenance intensive. Mogul #1 was rebuilt in the

AUTOMATIC BRAKE APPLIED

In the autumn of 1901, shopmen under Master Mechanic A. E. Allen began applying automatic air brake equipment. During August and September a large force of men installed air pumps, brake cylinders, air lines and hoses under the supervision of Harry Frasier of the Westinghouse Air Brake Company. These improvements were required by the Railway Safety Act of 1893, which later gave railroads a 10-year grace period.

General Manager John Hiskey (in doorway) talks with Johnnie Blossom and George Austin, as express shipments and baggage are loaded at Battle Mountain in about 1910. The *Silver State* is in the background. J.M. Hiskey collection; baggage cart sketch by Jim Scancarelli

The Safety Act also required that locomotives and rolling stock be equipped with automatic couplers. In 1902-04 NC workers began replacing older link-and-pin couplers with three-quarter-size Janney patent couplers.

The NC's three passenger cars were the first to receive the slotted-knuckle automatic couplers. Locomotive tenders were converted to the smaller size automatics, however, engines retained a long link coupler on the pilot beam until a federal inspector forced the NC to change them also. It would be several years before all of the remaining rolling stock was converted to the new couplers, and photos show a mix of link and pins as well as Janneys as late as 1907. Slotted knuckles allowed automatic couplers to mate with link and pins.

Employees on the NC often wore two or more hats, filling several different jobs on the railroad. Engineers Frank Dixon and J. H. Treat often worked in the shop when not running trains. Firemen Ed Merrill, Frank Bianchi, Ernest and Arthur Uren did likewise. Engineer Nelson Bartoo took over as master mechanic when A. E. Allen left.

MINES PROVIDE TRAFFIC
By 1903, Phelps Stokes' Nevada Mines Company at Berlin (55 miles south of Ledlie) and mining camps at Manhattan and Round Mountain, located further south in Big Smoky Valley, were providing fully one-third of the NC's freight traffic. However, the resurgence in mining was brief-lived, and by 1904 livestock shipments exceeded mineral and mining traffic.

On April 19, 1906 the *Battle Mountain Messenger* reported that the "Nevada Central's Saturday train had a rare double-header," with 14 cars, all loaded with 200 tons of machinery for the southern camps. The reporter noted that it had been "many a day since the NC train left Battle Mountain with that many cars." Shipments for the southern mines rode over the NC as far as Ledlie, where teamsters took over for the long, dusty haul to the camps. However, even this traffic had virtually ended by 1911.

Austin residents complained for years about the lack of daily mail service, which was carried by the NC on an alternating schedule of Monday-Wednesday-Friday. The Postal Department threatened to cancel the narrow gauge's lucrative mail contract. In order to provide daily service, the NC purchased a 12-passenger Shefield motor car, which arrived in November 1909.

The gasoline motor would begin a new era on the NC, which had its beginnings with an early 1880s steam-powered vehicle known as the "Go Devil."

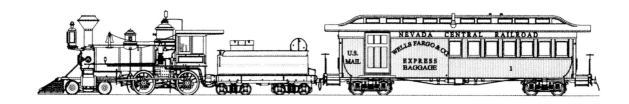

NC's reliable 4-4-0 #5 leads a mixed train across the desert soon after being equipped in 1901 with a Westinghouse air brake pump. It retains a link-and-pin coupler on the slatted pilot. C.W. Hauck collection

REBUILT MOGULS

BACK TO BASICS

Baldwin Mogul #2 emerged from the Battle Mountain shops in May 1901 (opposite top) with a slatted iron pilot, short smokebox, diamond stack, shiny new boiler jacket and fireman's side injector. An air pump was soon added to the fireman's side. C.M. Hollister from G.M. Best

Sister 2-6-0 #1 was rebuilt with shortened smokebox, diamond stack, extra injector and brass-bound boiler jacket. The One Spot waits at Battle Mountain (below) in c. 1900. She has not yet received an air pump. A Southern Pacific standard gauge train dwarfs narrow gauge cars at Battle Mountain (opposite lower) in 1903. Both, Ward Kimball collection

Number 1, enroute to Austin, pulls up to the water tank at Watts (above) in about 1903. Watts was one of only three stations between Battle Mountain and Clifton. The NC allowed local Shoshone Indians to ride free of charge (below), but made them ride on the tender or on freight cars...the NC was "all heart!" Both, Ward Kimball collection

BATTLE MOUNTAIN DEPOT

The Battle Mountain depot served both the Southern Pacific and NC and the two roads divided expenses. The station, pictured (above) in 1912, also served as an agency of Wells Fargo & Company Express and Western Union Telegraph. S.P. collection

Mogul #1, with a short mixed train, awaits departure from the south side of the depot (below) at the turn of the century. The sign reads "NEV. CENTRAL RR CO. TRAINS TO AUSTIN and all POINTS SOUTH." Ward Kimball collection

A long mixed train loads cattle at the Stiner Ranch, a mile north of Waters. Included in the consist are 10 stock cars, five box cars and a combine. Wally Trapnell collection

BAD NEWS AT BRIDGES

Mogul #1 has brought a rescue train to the scene of a derailment involving sister 2-6-0 #2 south of Bridges in about 1907. This is probably the wreck that Master Mechanic Dave Norris said occurred when a bull disputed the right-of-way at Mile Post 49 (Bobtown), resulting in the death of the bovine and derailment of the engine and seven cars. Badly smashed box car #209 ended its days as a cabin behind the Battle Mountain Shell Oil station. T.L. Williamson, NENM and J.M. Hiskey collection

DITCHED AGAIN...

Locomotive #1 was involved in a derailment similar to the one involving #2 on the previous pages. This occurred at Milepost 47 (below and opposite top), two miles north of Bobtown. The cause appears to have been a broken rail, and the results were the same...smashed cab and another trip to the backshops. The One Spot now sports an air compressor on the fireman's side, but retains a long coupling bar. A rescue train has arrived at the site of another derailment (opposite lower) near Canyon (MP 54) involving one of the combines.
All, Linwood Moody collection

Nevada Central's terminal at Clifton, located a mile below Austin, is pictured (above) in the early 1890s. Facilities included a small yard, depot, enginehouse and gallows turntable. The original water tank was located behind the camera, and the freighthouse and car shed had not yet been built. The Austin Mining Company's new mill is in the background. Ward Kimball collection

The red-painted depot (below) was photographed after the rails were removed in 1938 by Ted Wurm.

AUSTIN-CLIFTON

By June 1908, Clifton had a freighthouse next to the depot, a new water tank near the enginehouse and a new car shed. The Austin Mining Company's 40 stamp mill, in background, was built in 1890-91. It was connected with the deeper Lander Hill mines by the Austin-Manhattan drainage and haulage tunnel. Austin City Railway's grade runs above the silver mill. A baseball game is being played near the depot.
Author's collection

CHAPTER 9
HELL ON WHEELS

After 1890, silver and gold mining activities in Central Nevada began a steady decline. Steam train service over the Nevada Central was reduced to three roundtrip trains per week.

Throughout the 1890's, shopmen at Battle Mountain were busy converting old flats into new stock cars. By 1905 the line rostered 14 of the cattle conveniences. These conversions were rather crude affairs with no roofs—more like a stock pen on wheels. No two of these cattle cars were exactly alike.

By the early 1900s seasonal cattle and sheep movements exceeded mineral traffic, which had virtually ended by 1911. The area's last active mine had closed by 1913.

In 1901 John Merr Hiskey assumed the auditor's position for the railway at Battle Mountain. He would be deeply involved in the management of the struggling line and become the major factor in its survival for the next 38 years.

U.S. MAIL GLITCH
Austin residents continually complained to the Postal Service about the lack of daily mail over the narrow gauge.

Postal authorities threatened to pull the mail off of the Nevada Central unless something was done.

The answer was a 1907 two-cylinder, gasoline-powered Shefield motor car. The car could carry a dozen passengers, mail and small express shipments on days when regular mixed trains did not operate.

Nevada Central's timetable of July 1, 1908 called for three weekly mixed trains (one way on alternating days) with "additional daily mail and express service by railroad automobile." Austinites were pleased with the new service provided by Rail Motor #101.

The motor car was so successful that the railroad ordered a second similar Shefield from builder Fairbanks-Morse the following year. Motor #102 arrived in November 1909, just in time to take over the run, as Motor #101 had suffered mechanical problems that caused a suspension of daily service.

Motor #102 was slightly larger and more powerful than the #101. The *Reveille* remarked that "...she often arrived in Austin before noon, covering the 93 miles in three and a half hours." The June 30, 1909 timetable called the new vehicles the "Auto Mail."

Nevada Central's motor car #102 and its motorman pause at Battle Mountain (opposite) in about 1910. Herbert Merrill collection

The line's original Motor #101 (right) was a 4-wheel Shefield built by Fairbanks-Morse in 1907. Jerry Mock collection

THE "GO DEVIL"

The gasoline-powered motor cars were not the first attempts to provide a self-propelled substitute for a steam-powered train on the Nevada Central. That honor goes to a unique early steam car known as the "Go Devil."

In 1885, the narrow gauge received national attention with an April 30 article in *Railway Age*. The industry newspaper called the NC's Go Devil a great novelty and a very lively machine.

The four-wheel steam car featured a small vertical boiler, double 4 3/8" x 4 7/8" inch cylinders, a 40-gallon water tank and a 150-pound capacity coal bin, upon which an operator and passenger could sit. The entire mechanism sat on a wooden frame and weighed about 2,000 pounds.

The Go Devil was built in 1882-3 by Master Mechanic Z.T. Sprigg and Boilermaker T.F. Godfrey in the Battle Mountain machine shop. It was intended for use by the roadmaster and was noted as being the only one of its kind in the West.

SNORTING AND DASHING

The small cylinders were inside—connected to 24"-inch diameter drive wheels. Virginia City's *Territorial Enterprise*, Mark Twain's old newspaper, noted that at some 400 rpm, the steam car "goes snorting and wildly dashing over the road at 35 mph." It had no trouble climbing the 350-feet-per-mile Battle Mountain & Lewis grade.

After some modifications by newly-appointed Master Mechanic Gilchrist, the Go Devil was tested on the steep Austin City Ry. grade out of Clifton. The changes involved lowering the small (42" high) boiler's top flue sheet and adding iron straps to reinforce the wooden frame.

Following the initial excitement over the Go Devil, it received only brief mention in local newspapers over the next few years. On March 27, 1889 Superintendent C.W. Hinchcliffe used the steam machine on a roundtrip to Battle Mountain from Austin. Two years later Brass Hat Hinchcliffe and T.H. George made a nine-hour roundtrip out of Battle Mountain in April 1891. It was again noted as being in service in October of 1892.

There is an unconfirmed report of the steam motor being owned or used by the Manhattan Silver Mining Company, owners of the Austin City Railway. However, the mining firm had closed down its Austin mines, mill, concentrator and railway by mid-1893.

The Go Devil is not mentioned again by the media or in NC records after the mid-1890s. Its remains were reported on a sagebrush sidetrack as late as 1930.

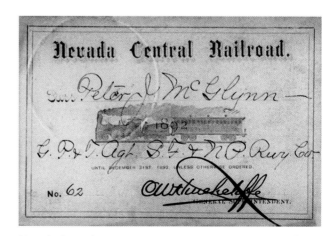

Nevada Central's steam motor was quite an innovation when built in 1882-83 at Battle Mountain by Master Mechanic Z.T. Sprigg and Boilermaker T.F. Godfrey. The unique Go Devil received national attention from *Railway Age* in 1885. Sketch of the machine is by Jim Scancarelli. The 1892 NC pass is from the author's files.

Shortly after the new Shefield Motor #102 arrived in mid-November 1909, the Big Flood of February 1910 washed out five miles of track near Baileys. The flood took out several large trestles, and the entire NC was shut down until repairs could be completed in late April. Washouts, floods and winter snow blockades were becoming annual affairs.

John Merr Hiskey was named general manager of the NC in 1913. Business began to improve shortly after Hiskey took over. He would eventually wear a number of other hats including superintendent, secretary, treasurer and auditor. Hiskey was the reason the narrow gauge ran as long and as well as it did.

Anson Phelps Stokes died in 1913, leaving the Nevada Central Railroad and his Nevada Company mining holdings to his son John G. Phelps Stokes. The younger Stokes, in town for a NC annual meeting, later purchased the mine under and around his former Stokes Castle residence.

NEW MOTOR #103

Meanwhile, the shop completed Motor #103 under the supervision of Master Mechanic Nelson E. Bartoo. The new car was built along the lines of Motor #102, but slightly larger. The car was built using parts from Fairbanks-Morse and was painted maroon with a dark green interior. It made its first run on January 17, 1914. In later years the #103 received a Model A Ford engine and was so hard to start that crews called her the "Bull of the Woods."

Motors #102 and #103 resumed the alternating daily Auto Mail service. Steam trains were operated only when necessary. The *Messenger* of Battle Mountain noted the shipment of 10 cars of cattle on April 4, 1914. That fall the paper said that 55 carloads of sheep and cattle had come into town during the first 10 days of November. An additional stock car was built in 1915.

Motor #102 was rebuilt with a new body during 1914, leaving the new #103 to handle all the work. When Motor #103 was down for repairs, the mail did not go through, much to the consternation of Austin residents. On February 21, 1914 the NC promised, "Daily mail will resume next week." However, service did not resume again until mid-March.

A broken rail "ditched" a mixed train and its combination car on November 26, 1914. The *Messenger* reported that the coach was "practically demolished." While the article did not specify what combine was involved, it appears to have been #2. In January 1916, Carman Jack Kelley was noted to be still repairing the cars that were damaged.

NEVADA SHORT LINE CAR

During 1914, Master Mechanic Bartoo supervised construction of a motor car for the nearby Nevada Short Line Railway. This new narrow gauge ran from Oreana, on the Southern Pacific, 12 miles south to silver mines in Rochester Canyon. The NSL Motor was similar to Nevada Central's #103 and was built in the Reno shops of the Nevada-California-Oregon. The Motor made its first run on January 22, 1915 but was derailed and wrecked in Rochester Canyon in March 1916.

J. D. Norris was named the NC's new master mechanic in March 1916. He replaced Nelson Bartoo, who had been badly injured in an accident.

In the autumn of 1920, General Manager Hiskey traveled to Denver and purchased former Argentine & Grays Peak Motor #9 from Morse Brothers Machinery & Supply Company. This railbus had been built by the Vulcan Iron Works in 1917 and was powered by a six-cylinder, 100-h.p. Wisconsin gasoline motor.

The Battle Mountain shops drastically rebuilt the former Colorado motor car, adding a new body and rear baggage doors. It was painted maroon and lettered NC #104. The new #104 was 33 feet long and weighed 20,000 pounds, heaviest of all the NC's motors. Its Lecce-Neville starter-generator was a big advantage over hand cranking. But, despite an investment of more than $6,300 the #104 was expensive to operate and only saw a few years of regular service.

An advertisement in the July 16, 1920 issue of *Railway Age* offered Nevada Short Line #1, an 1879 Baldwin 2-6-0, for sale at $3,000 FOB Oreana, Nevada. The NSL engine had previously served the Utah & Northern and Golconda & Adelaide railroads. In November, Vice President James W. McCulloch authorized John Hiskey's purchase of the locomotive, which became NC's Six Spot. It is not known what the NC paid for the aging Mogul, but it was insured for $1,000 on February 1, 1922.

A strong wind blew over the Nevada Central's coach-house in 1922. The *Silver State* and a combine inside were found lying on their sides, but were not badly damaged.

TYPICAL SCHEDULE

The August 1924 schedule was typical for the period. It called for motor runs to Austin on Monday and Wednesday departing Battle Mountain at 9:15 a.m. and arriving at 2:15 p.m. Mixed trains left Battle Mountain on Friday at 9:15 a.m. and arrived Austin at 3:15 p.m. The Saturday mixed left Austin at 8:15 a.m. and was scheduled back in Battle Mountain at 2:00 p.m. The Motors returned to Battle Mountain on Tuesday and Thursday, departing Austin at 8:15 a.m. and arriving home at 1:00 p.m. Even with three motor cars and a once-a-week roundtrip mixed train, the NC was unable to provide daily mail, passenger and express service in each direction. A notation on the timetable stated, "Steam trains will not exceed 16 miles per hour and will observe time of departure from terminal only."

A rare doubleheader ran in early August 1924. The *Messenger* reported that the train carried 26 cars of coal and merchandise, plus a combination car.

The Nevada Central ordered two new railbuses from A. Meister & Son of Sacramento in 1925. Motor #105 arrived

THE NEVADA CENTRAL RAILROAD Co.

No. 22   TIME TABLE   No. 22

EFFECTIVE WEDNESDAY, JUNE 30TH, 1909, AT 6 O'CLOCK A. M.

MOUNTAIN (S. P.) TIME.

This Time Table is for the Government and use of Employes only, and the right to vary it, without notice, is reserved.

TRAINS GOING SOUTH.		Length of Siding in No. of Cars.	Distance from Austin.	STATIONS and SIDINGS.	Distance from Battle Mountain	Telegraph Calls.	Station Nos.	TRAINS GOING NORTH.	
No. 53	No. 1							No. 2.	No. 54.
AUTO MAIL Leaving MONDAYS. WEDNESDAYS. & FRIDAYS.	ACCOMODA-TION. Leaving TUESDAYS. THURSDAYS. & SATURDAYS.							ACCOMODA-TION. Leaving WEDNESDAYS. FRIDAYS. & SUNDAYS.	AUTO MAIL Leaving TUESDAYS. THURSDAYS. & SATURDAYS.
Depart 8.00 A. M.	Depart 8.30 A.M.	300 D	93.3	**BATTLE MOUNTAIN**† Y 11	BM S		0	Arrive. 2.30 P. M.	Arrive 2.30 P. M.
	9.12 "	12 N	82.3	*LEWIS 3.4	11	JC	11	1.55 "	
	9.25 "		78.9	*DILLON 4.6	14.4	DN	14	1.40 "	
	9.40 "	3 N	74.3	*BAILEYS 16.6	19	BY	19	1.20 "	
	10.45 "	10 S	57.7	*WATTS† 7.9	35.6	WS	35	12.30 "	
	11.13 "	6 S	49.8	* BRIDGES 10.5	43.5	BD	43	12.02 "	
	12 00 noon	16 N	39.3	*CANYON 2.1	54	CN	54	11.30 A. M.	
	12.10 P.M.		37.2	* WALTERS 4.5	56.1	W	56	11.21 "	
	12.30 "	5 N	32.7	*RAVENSWOOD 2 3	60.6	WD	61	11.06 "	
	12.40 "	10 S	30.4	*VAUGHN'S† 7.2	62.9	VA	63	10.58 "	
	1.15 "	20 S	23.2	* SILVER CREEK† 4.4	70.1	SC	70	10.28 "	
	1.35 "	10 S	18.8	*CATON'S 11.7	74.5	CA	74	10.10 "	
	2.20 "	30 D	7.1	*LEDLIE † Y 7.1	86.2	JN	86	9.30 "	
3.00 P. M. Arrive.	3.00 P.M Arrive.	40 D		**AUSTIN** † O	93.3	MC GO Z	93	9.00 " Depart.	8.30 A M Depart

No. 53 will clear time of No. 2. between Austin and Battle Mountain.

No. 54 will clear time of No. 1, 30 minutes between Battle Mountain and Canyon 30 minutes at Canyon 40 minutes between Canyon and Silver Creek 1 hour between Silver Creek and Austin

Southbound trains will be considered superior to Northbound trains of the same class.

No. 1 has right of track over No. 2.   **Nos. 1 and 2 have right over Nos. 53 and 54.**

Trains Must Not Exceed Twenty Miles per Hour Under Any Circumstances.

☞ Flag Stations.   ⊣ Water Tanks.   § Telegraph wire not cut in.   ( ) Turn Table.   Y Wye.   ) Double End Switch.

N Stub switch connected north.   S Stub Switch connected south.

Conductors and Enginemen must see that they are supplied with lamps, flags, tools, etc., and have train made up and ready to leave thirty minutes before leaving time.

All trains will register at AUSTIN and BATTLE MOUNTAIN.   IN CASE OF DOUBT, ALWAYS TAKE THE SAFE SIDE.

J. G. PHELPS STOKES,
President.

J. M. HISKEY,
Superintendent.

The Nevada Central Railroad's "Auto Mail" gasoline motors and steam-powered mixed train "Accommodations" appear on this June 30, 1909 timetable. Ward Kimball collection

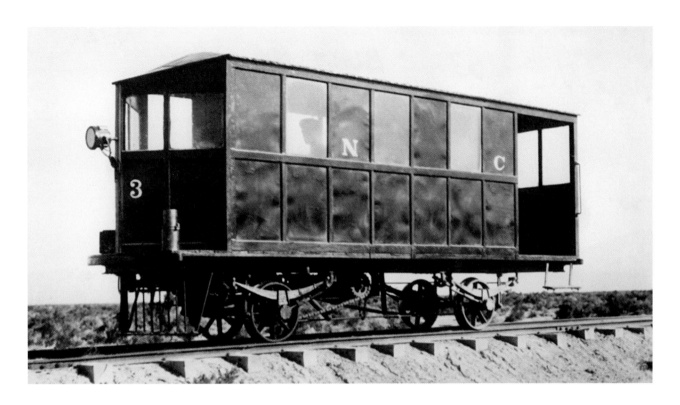

A NEW MOTOR...

New Shefield Motor #103 was built in the Nevada Central shops in 1914 using Fairbanks Morse parts and a Ford engine. It was painted maroon with a green interior. Author's collection

in Battle Mountain in December, but was not put into service immediately, due to having been damaged while enroute. The 4-cylinder Ford-powered #105 made her first trip in March. The new motor was 23 feet long and 7 feet wide. It carried the rear-mounted engine on a steel frame and weighed in at 6,800 pounds.

BUILT-IN TURNTABLE

Motor #106 arrived in late March 1926. It was similar to sister #105, except for being three feet longer and having an extra set of wheels behind the rear driving axle. The #106 had a slightly more powerful 6-cylinder Buda engine. Both of the Meister railbuses had a built-in turntable, allowing them to be turned in place.

A major consideration in the purchase of the two new Meister motors was the pending completion of the Lincoln Highway (U.S. 50) between Ely and Fallon. The highway, which ran through Austin, gave the narrow gauge more competition from trucks and buses. Hiskey felt that the two motors would be able to attract passengers, express

and provide reliable daily mail. The balance sheet for 1925 showed a loss for the year of $10,597.

Soon after Meister Motors #105 and #106 entered service, older Motor #104 was relegated to standby status and seldom used. A large corrugated iron car barn was added to the east end of the Battle Mountains shops to house the motors. The deficit for 1926 was only $900.

Engineer and Motorman Herbert "Henhouse" Merrill said, "I always carried a two day lunch, and what I did not eat the first day was left in either the motor car or locomotive," adding that he never knew for sure when he would make it back home. "Home" for "Henhouse" was caboose #10, where he had a bunk and a coal stove for cooking and heat. "Besides," Merrill added, "the local flophouse had bed bugs."

CHARTER AMENDED

General Manager Hiskey reported that despite the large investment in the two Meister-built motors, they proved to be unsuitable for the narrow gauge's operating condi-

...AND NOT SO NEW ENGINE

Former Nevada Short Line #1 had a number of owners prior to becoming NC #6 in 1922. Railway Age, from Kyle Wyatt

tions. With highway competition increasing, the directors amended the NC's charter in order to allow the railroad to operate a bus line.

John Hiskey then purchased a highway bus for the Nevada Central. The first run between Fallon and Ely was made on April 27, 1927. On October 21, Hiskey bought out the competing Fallon-Ely Stage Line from George C. Coverston. A new company, the Nevada Central Motor Lines, took over in late 1927. Despite the official name, everyone referred to the bus line as the "Hiskey Stage."

Motor #102 was hit by a state-owned gravel truck at the Lincoln Highway grade crossing west of Austin on December 21, 1928. Jesse Treat, the motorman, was injured, but two female passengers were unharmed. Hiskey reported that the motor was "demolished, burned and a total loss."

With Motor #102 destroyed and the two Meister units so unreliable, older Motor #103 was left to uphold any attempts at "irregular service." The #102 was replaced by a converted Model AA Ford truck that the shop crews rebuilt for rail use in 1929. The one-and-a-half-ton truck had been purchased new by the Hiskey Stage in 1928. Cost of Nevada Central's new Motor #107 was covered by a $2,000 insurance settlement from the state for the Motor #102 accident.

MOTOR TRADED

Motor #105 was traded to the nearby Eureka-Nevada Railway for two side dump gondola cars (E-N #301, #302) in 1931. The E-N rebuilt the old #105 as their Motor #23. Motor #103 and Truck #107 were used thereafter by the NC. Former Argentine & Grays Peak Motor #104 was scrapped in 1934.

Wages were cut during the Great Depression years and no further attempt was made to provide the long-promised "daily mail, passenger and express service." John Hiskey, in a letter to the board of directors, wrote, "Mail service will be operated by old motors and no effort will be made to provide regular, attractive passenger accommodations."

By the 1930s, only about 30 steam-powered trains were operated each year and most of these were seasonal livestock shipments. The NC had simply given up!

A Nevada Central Motor Lines Cadillac has stopped at Austin's International Hotel in 1928. The bus line was known as the "Hiskey Stage." The hotel was moved here from Virginia City in 1862. Nevada Historical Society

Motor #104 came from Colorado's mountain climbing Argentine & Grays Peak in 1920. The late Gilbert Kneiss found it at Battle Mountain (above) in September 1938. Arnold Menke collection

Ted Wurm photographed the #104 in a shed in June that year.

MOTOR #105 TO EUREKA-NEVADA

Nevada Central's motor car #105, built by A. Meister & Son in 1925, was traded to the nearby Eureka-Nevada Railway for a pair of side-dump gondolas in 1931. It became E-N #23 and is shown at Palisade in the late 1930s. Ted Wurm

MEISTER MOTOR #106

Motor #106 came new from A. Meister & Son in 1926 and was painted red, green and yellow. The heavy Meister motors saw limited use and spent much of their time in the shop. T.L. Williamson, Ted Wurm

A Hiskey Stage bus meets Meister #106 in early 1930s. Linwood Moody collection

BULL OF THE WOODS

After homemade motor #103 received a Model A Ford engine, she was so hard to crank that crews called her the "Bull of the Woods." The #103 was equipped with a snowplow pilot (left and below) in the 1930s. Both, Robert W. Brown collection

Pictured inside the enginehouse addition (lower left), it continued in service until the end of operations. Jerry Mock, Greg Maxwell collection

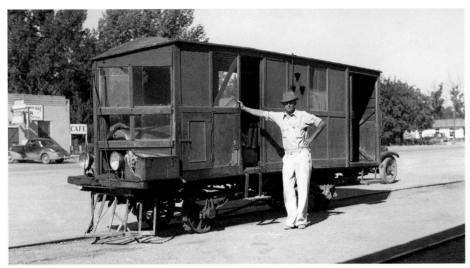

Motor #103 hauled the mail, express and a few passengers on the 93-mile run between Battle Mountain and Austin for many years. It was the most dependable motor on the line. The #103 is shown with its motorman (left) at Battle Mountain and returning from Austin in May 1937. Linwood Moody, SMU DeGolyer Library and Gilbert Kneiss

The Nevada Central's last motor, #107, was a 1928 Ford stake body truck converted for rail use in 1929 after motor #102 was destroyed in a grade crossing accident. The #107 is pictured (right) near the shops in April 1938. Walt Young, Bob Brown collection

It waits behind the Battle Mountain depot (below) in 1936. Arnold Menke collection

CHAPTER 10
RUST & ALKALI DUST

 THROUGHOUT THE 1920S AND 1930S the NC struggled along against seemingly impossible odds with aging equipment. Gone was the once lucrative gold and silver mining traffic.

Each winter saw cold temperatures, often accompanied by snowdrifts that packed canyon cuts and blockaded the line for days at a time. Spring often saw the normally placid Reese River raging out of its banks, washing out trestles, bridges and trackage.

The springtime also saw sheep being transported to summer pastures, providing a little revenue for the struggling carrier. July could bring temperatures in excess of 100 degrees, accompanied by sunkinks that derailed trains. Fall was the time for stock shipments with extra crews and an occasional doubleheaded train, it was the one good season for the NC.

STOCK RUN ACTIVITY
The spring and autumn stock rush saw the greatest activity on the sagebrush narrow gauge. Everyone pitched in to get the job done. Men who were normally employed in the shops became trainmen.

The day began with an empty string of cattle cars leaving Battle Mountain about 4:00 a.m. for livestock loading pens at Ravaughns, Ledlie and the ranches along the route. The larger ranches shipping sheep and cattle included Malloy's, Welche's, Potts Brothers, Phillppe's, Abels' and John Labora.

Time was an important factor for these livestock trains, and a loaded consist would rush back to Battle Mountain's stock corral by noon, in order to feed and water the animals before they were transferred to standard gauge cars. The NC's stock yard was located just east of the shops at the tail end of the wye.

While the NC was built through the generally level high desert and canyon country, there were several "hills" that train crews had to battle. Ten miles south of Battle Mountain, near Lewis Junction, was "Twenty Mile Hill." This section had 10 miles of southbound upgrade to Baileys, followed by three miles of downhill running. "Twenty-Six Mile Hill" involved a steeper grade near Helena, then a level section to beyond Bridges, followed by seven more miles of steep, curving trackage through the Reese River Canyon.

TWISTING GRADE
The Reese River Canyon, 55 miles south, contained several miles of twisting grade through cuts and a bridge over the river that was continually threatened by flood waters. Smaller trestles bridged side canyons and dry creeks. The normally placid and often dry Reese was subject to annual flooding due to rapid snow melts and cloudbursts that brought rocks, sand and mud down side canyons. These yearly rampages plagued the railroad throughout its lifetime. Most notable were the Reese River floods of 1901, 1909 and 1910. These floods washed out bridges and tracks, and shut down the line for months.

The "Six Mile Grade" began at Ledlie and included a steady 2% climb to Clifton. Steam trains were often required to break their train and double the hill.

In 1922 the NC Railroad purchased its last "new" steam locomotive. Mogul #6 had been built by Baldwin in 1879. It was purchased by General Manager Hinchcliffe from the recently-abandoned Nevada Short Line where it was #1. The 2-6-0 had previously run as Utah & Northern #13, Oregon Short Line & Utah Northern #17 and Golconda & Adelaide #1. The locomotive would go on to greater fame and preservation.

It was not the first time the elderly Baldwin had been to Battle Mountain. *The Messenger* reported on January 26, 1898, "The locomotive for the narrow gauge from Golconda to the copper mines passed through Thursday night." It was, of course, loaded aboard a standard gauge car on a westbound Southern Pacific freight. The Golconda & Adelaide Railroad was in operation a year later, hauling copper ore to the smelter.

FOUR STEAM LOCOMOTIVES

The NC now had four serviceable Baldwin steamers: 1881 Moguls #1 and #2, 1875 4-4-0 #5 and the "new" 1879 2-6-0 #6. Gasoline motor cars provided most of the daily action as one or two locomotives were usually undergoing repairs in the shop.

After the mid-1920s, the Clifton water tank was out of service, often requiring engines to run for water at the Ledlie tank. An extra water tender was sometimes added behind locomotives #2 and #5 during times when tanks ran dry or were under repair.

The late 1920s saw a resurgence of mining in Copper Canyon, nine miles from Dillon (MP 14). A platform of crossties was built at trackside where Fred Uren hand shoveled the copper ore into NC cars. The ore was shipped to a smelter near Salt Lake City, Utah. Gold ore from the McCoy Mine in Buffalo Valley was hauled to Baileys (MP 19). However, the mineral traffic was short-lived.

During the first 20 days of September 1927, the narrow gauge brought 102 carloads of cattle and 105 cars of sheep to the Battle Mountain corral. This was quite a challenge for a railroad with only 14 serviceable open-top stock cars.

The narrow gauge had essentially given up hope of maintaining any sort of daily passenger or mail service and

began its own bus line in 1927. The Nevada Central Motor Lines ran from Ely through Austin to Fallon over the new Lincoln Highway (U.S. 50). It was known locally as the "Hiskey Stage," a throwback to the days when Wells, Fargo & Co. stage coaches traveled the route.

Nevada Central Railroad's newest old locomotive, #6, was taken out of service for repairs on October 8, 1927. It had only been used for five years, and photographs of it in action are rare.

MOGUL #1 SET ASIDE

Mogul (2nd) #1, which had not been used since late 1923, was finally set aside for scrapping in 1931. It would be robbed of parts to keep sister #2 in service. The One Spot sat resting and rusting near the Battle Mountain shops for the next seven years. This left only Mogul #2 and American Standard #5 to power the line's steam trains, which ran on average only about two or three times each month.

John Hiskey was forced to cut wages during the Great Depression in order to keep the NC going. Stanley Estes, who hired out as a fireman and shopman in the early 1930s, had his pay cut from $4 a day to $3 during the hard times. Estes said that even with the long hours, he "was happy to have a regular job." The entire nation was affected, although the narrow gauge had been in its own depression for many years. As a cost-cutting move, the Clifton depot was closed during this period.

The railroad was shut down for two months in early 1932 due to ice and snow. New Motor (truck) #107 was fitted with an iron snowplow pilot, but often could not gain enough traction to break through drifts and complete its run over icy rails.

RESCUE TRAIN SENT

Motorman Herbert "Henhouse" Merrill was stranded while trying to buck snow with Motor #107 two miles south of Bridges (MP 43). The temperature was 20 degrees below zero, and the motor was not heated. Herbert was able to hook up his portable telephone to the trackside line and contact the Battle Mountain shop just before the men went home at 5:00 p.m. Fortunately, the line had not been taken out by the storm. It required several hours to build up steam on a cold locomotive. "Henhouse" thought he might freeze before the rescue train arrived.

BLAST THROUGH SNOW

With Superintendent Dave Norris at the throttle, and Fireman Bianchi blasting through 45 miles of drifted snow-covered track, the men thought Merrill might be frozen to death before they could reach him. Arriving at the stalled motor around 2:30 a.m., they found "Henhouse" alive, but very cold. They brought out a pint of whiskey and poured a tin cup full before taking him to the caboose to thaw out.

After his near-death adventure, Merrill talked Hiskey into buying small coal-burning heaters for the motors. Motor #105, which the railroad purchased new from A. Meister & Son in 1925, was traded to the nearby Eureka-Nevada Railway (formerly Eureka & Palisade) for a pair of side-dump gondolas in 1931. Motor #104 was scrapped in 1934 and Meister #106 was seldom used and sat derelict near the Battle Mountain shops. This left only homemade Motor #103 and rail-mounted Ford Motor #107 in operation.

The handwriting was on the wall by the time of the September 20, 1937 stockholders and directors annual meeting. The NC had a "marginal existence" for many years and could not continue. It was time to call it quits.

The NC had struggled through the high desert sagebrush and canyon country, where cows outnumbered people, for 57 years. There were no towns along its 93-mile route. The railroad had enjoyed 32 profitable years, intermixed with 25 years of losses. It never paid a dividend on its common stock and no interest on its bonds since 1917. The narrow gauge was said to have never killed anyone...only scared a few people half to death!

An application for abandonment was made to the Interstate Commerce Commission following the annual meeting. Approval was granted on December 20, 1937.

The Nevada Central's tracks head south across the sage-covered desert (opposite page) in July 1938. Lennox Photo, Al Phelps collection

Mogul #6, the newest and last addition to the steam roster, had a number of different owners before coming to the NC in 1922. UC Bancroft Library

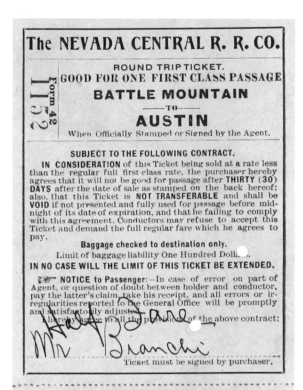

American Standard #5 sits at the east end addition to the Battle Mountain enginehouse in 1936.

Herbert "Henhouse" Merrill nearly froze to death aboard motor #107 while trying to buck through snow drifts near Bridges in 20-below-zero temperatures. *Walt Young, Bob Brown collection*

American Standard #5 heads a long string of stock cars, trailed by a caboose (above) in the late 1930s. The crew poses with the 1876 Baldwin (below) at the corrugated iron enginehouse (east end addition) in 1936. The #5 received a new Baldwin boiler in 1910. Linwood Moody collection

Baldwin 2-6-0 #2 (2nd) had a long career on the NC. It was modified, rebuilt and changed over the years, receiving a new boiler in 1914. But, the Two Spot ended its years looking much as it had when built in 1881. It was under steam at Battle Mountain (left) in 1922 and still active there (below) in the late 1930s.
Fred Jukes, Gilbert Kneiss

BATTLE MOUNTAIN...

Battle Mountain's Main Street (lower left) faced the Nevada Central tracks and the joint depot (below). Number 5 switches there (lower right) in the 1930s. Clockwise from top: author, SP, Wally Trapnell and Linwood Moody collections

THE SHOP AREA

Harp switchstands (left) and three-way stub switches (below) were common in the 1880s, but rare by the late 1930s. The structures are (left to right) office, enginehouse, water tank, car shop, rip track area and stores building. Note the unusual iron switchstand.
Richard B. Jackson

SWITCHING BATTLE MOUNTAIN

Mogul #2 switches a Standard Oil tank car at Battle Mountain (above and below), near the end of operations. Author's collection

The silver-painted tank cars (above) were owned by the oil company, and they later went to the Nevada County Narrow Gauge. Ted Wurm and Author's collection

Cars of gasoline are switched at the Standard oil plant (below) at Clifton on August 14, 1937. C.P. Ross, USGS

STOCK CARS...COBBLED TOGETHER

Nevada Central stock cars were generally open top affairs, built in the Battle Mountain car shop from existing flats. Two of these "cobbled" cars are switched on the hillside (left) at Clifton in 1937. C.P. Ross, USGS

More refined stock car #60 (middle) was built from a taper-sill flat, had a roof and single spring trucks. Bob Brown collection

Open top stock #154 (bottom) was a typical 8-ton car used in the last years. Richard B. Jackson

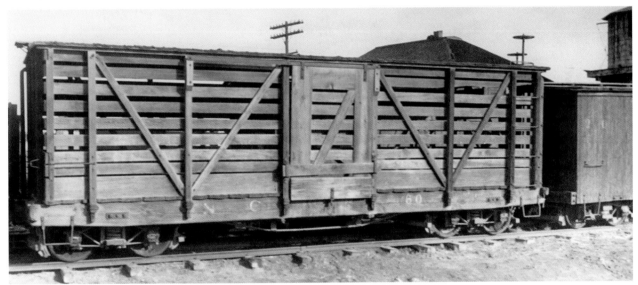

THE END IS NEAR

The ice-encrusted Battle Mountain tank (left), located near the enginehouse, was a 1912 replacement for the original tank of 1880. The tank itself measured 14 feet in diameter and was 10 feet high. Bob Brown collection

Mogul #2 sits in the enginehouse door (below), next to the water tank. Guy L. Dunscomb

THE NEVADA CENTRAL RAILROAD CO.

GENERAL OFFICE

J. M. HISKEY,
GENERAL MANAGER

AUSTIN, NEVADA.

FILE

THE NEVADA CENTRAL RAILROAD COMPANY.

NOTICE OF ANNUAL MEETING.

The Annual meeting of the Stockholders of The
Nevada Central Railroad Company, for the elec-
tion of Directors for the ensuing year, will be
held at the office of the Company, at Austin,
Lander County, Nevada, on Monday, September 20,
1937, 4:00 PM.

Transfer books will close Friday, Sept.10,1937.

J. G. Phelps Stokes,
President.

John M. Hiskey,
Secretary.

Dated at Austin, Nevada, Aug. 15, 1937.

First publication, Aug. 15, 1937
Last publication, Sept. 18, 1937.

THE LAST TRAIN

The last Nevada Central annual meeting was held on September 20, 1937 (left). Here it was decided to abandon the narrow gauge. ICC approval came on December 20. The last regular train to Austin (below) on January 2, 1938, drew little attention. These two snapshots show it passing as a small boy seems to be the only interested observer. Jerry Mock collection

CHAPTER 11

SUNSET ON THE NARROW GAUGE

FOLLOWING APPROVAL of the Nevada Central Railroad's abandonment petition by the Interstate Commerce Commission on December 20, 1937, General Manager John Merr Hiskey made plans to end 57 years of narrow gauge operations.

In the previous five years the line had sold an average of only four passenger fares each month and had not carried a single local freight shipment. Carload freight amounted to 156 loads each year from 1933 to 1937.

The NC's charter expired on February 1, 1938 and Mogul #2 pulled the last regular train out of Austin (Clifton) the next day. Unlike the canon fire, torchlight parade and excitement of the first train back in 1880, there was no fanfare whatsoever for the last train. The event was virtually unrecorded, save for a pair of small drugstore prints in a family album.

FIND JOBS

Several railroaders found employment on the Nevada County Narrow Gauge out of Grass Valley, California. Others found jobs on ranches, but most moved away from the area. The NCNG jobs did not last long as this line was abandoned in 1942.

The rails and most of the equipment were sold to the Hyman-Michaels Company (United Commercial Company) of San Francisco for $17,500. The first rails were lifted at Clifton on April 20, 1938. Through the efforts of the late Gilbert Kneiss, the private car *Silver State* was donated to the Railway & Locomotive Historical Society's Pacific Coast Chapter. Hyman-Michaels then gave locomotive #6 and combine #2 to the society.

Mogul #2 pulled scrap trains throughout the summer on an ever-decreasing basis, and the scrappers brought in a four-wheel Whitcomb 0-4-0 to finish tearing up the line. The 20-ton gas-mechanical engine had previously been

The sun is about to set on the Sagebrush Narrow Gauge, as trusty 1881 Mogul #2 makes up a train during 1938 scrapping operations. Linwood Moody collection

used by Spanish Peak Lumber at Quincy, California and the Swayne Lumber Company of Oroville, California.

STRUCTURES FOR SALE
On September 18, 1938 General Manager Hiskey put up for sale all structures, stock pens, water tanks, windmills, bridges and trestles. The list included depots at Austin (Clifton) and Ledlie, water tanks at Ledlie, Vaughns, Watts and Dillon and the Battle Mountain shop complex.

The Battle Mountain shop buildings included the original shop, machine shop, blacksmith shop, locomotive shed, car repair shop and supply room. All of these wooden structures were joined together.

The east end addition's locomotive shed measured 60' x 60' with 18'-high side walls. The addition was of frame construction, covered with galvanized, corrugated iron siding and roof (approximately 10,000 square feet). Also included in the sale was an oil house, tool house, assorted tools, jacks and a hand-winch derrick with an 8'x 8' boom and mast.

The final rails were pulled up on September 27, 1938. At this time there was little interest in the old tickets, forms, waybills, train sheets, passes, paperwork and other records of the faded line. Local rumor says that Hiskey ordered these records dumped down a mine shaft near the Stokes' Castle in Austin.

That fall, Hiskey offered to sell the line's remaining locomotives, 2-6-0 #2 and 4-4-0 #5. Disney animator Ward Kimball, with help from Gilbert Kneiss, friends Gerald M. Best and Richard B. Jackson, was able to purchase #2 in late 1938. Hiskey personally kept ownership of the former North Pacific Coast 4-4-0.

EUREKA-NEVADA DIES
On September 21, 1938, the Eureka-Nevada Railroad at Palisade, some 50 miles east of Battle Mountain, was abandoned. This high desert three-foot-gauge operated through similar territory to the fading mining town of Eureka. Built as the Eureka & Palisade in 1875, the 90-mile line suffered a similar fate when mining declined in the 1890s.

The same 1910 floods that washed out the NC did even worse damage on the E&P, putting 30 miles of trackage under water. Rebuilt in 1912 as the Eureka-Nevada, motor cars handled much of the line's passenger, mail and express in the final years. John E. Sexton kept this narrow gauge in business, much as John Hiskey had done on the NC.

John Hiskey, who retained ownership of 1876 4-4-0 #5, leased his engine to a representative of the Golden Gate International Exposition. The agreement had a provision that made the R&LHS's Pacific Coast Chapter responsible for the engine's care.

NC's 4-4-0 #5, 2-6-0 #6, combine #1 and coach *Silver State* were loaded aboard standard gauge cars in December of 1938. They were taken to the Western Pacific's Oakland Shops where they would be overhauled for use at the exposition.

The pageant planned to open in 1939 on Treasure Island in San Francisco Bay. The refurbished and repainted equipment would steam on stage in a re-enactment of the Gold Spike "Wedding of the Rails" between the Union Pacific and Central Pacific at Promontory Summit on May 10, 1869.

LIVES ON
While the Nevada Central Railroad was now a thing of the past, the railroad would live on, not only in fading memories and photographs, but in tangible examples of its motive power and rolling stock. Because of the far sighted efforts of pioneer rail historians like Kneiss, Best and Kimball, the sun has never really set on the Sagebrush Narrow Gauge.

Number 2, the former *Sidney Dillon* of the 1880s, steams near the Battle Mountain shops (above) before leaving for end-of-track on June 24, 1938. Richard B. Jackson

Number 2, with an auxiliary tender from Mogul #6, takes water (below), before heading out that July. Author's collection

A scrap train readies for departure (opposite top) on April 22, 1938. Linwood Moody collection

Number 2 steams behind the shops (below) and backs away from the Battle Mountain station (opposite below), on June 24, 1938. Richard B. Jackson

With a full coal load and auxiliary tender from Engine #6, the Two Spot (above) is ready to pull a scrapper's train in April 1938. Ted Gay

Another train load of 1870's and 1880's 35-pound rail steams into Battle Mountain (above) in 1938. H.H. Fulton

Repaired Engine #2 hauls a scrap train into town (below) that June. Richard B. Jackson

Mogul #2 has broken a siderod (above) near the Reese River in May 1938. Gilbert Kneiss

Workers transfer rails (below) to standard gauge flats. T.L. Williamson

Hyman-Michaels brought in a small Whitcomb gas locomotive (c/n 12205-6/1926) to finish scrapping the NC. It had previously been used on the Spanish Peak Lumber. Co. (CA 1926-1933), then on Swayne Lumber. Co. (CA 1936). The 0-4-0 was later standard gauged in order to scrap the Deep Creek RR (UT) and is now at the Rio Vista Railroad Museum. Linwood Moody collection

Nevada Central's One Spot was not used after 1923. It sat in the Battle Mountain yards (above) and was scrapped (below) in
1938. Arnold Menke collection

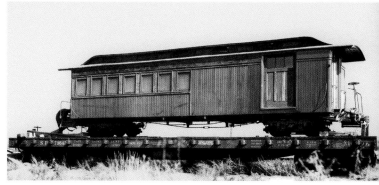

The Nevada Central lasted long enough for its antique cars and engines to be preserved. Mogul #2 went to Ward Kimball, combine #1, the *Silver State* and 4-4-0 #5 all went to the Railway & Locomotive Historical Society, along with 2-6-0 #6, shown loaded in a standard gauge gondola. C.W. Witbeck, Linwood Moody and Arnold Menke collections

The Battle Mountain shop complex was photographed from the main line looking north (above) in June 1938. Bob Dockery collection

Piles of 35-pound rail, some dating from the 1870s, await removal (lower left) in late 1938. By 1940 (lower right) little was left. Linwood Moody collection

CHAPTER 12
RESTORATION & PRESERVATION

PLANS WERE BEING MADE for the Golden Gate International Exposition, scheduled to open in 1939 on Treasure Island, in San Francisco Bay. The Exposition would include an historical pageant entitled Cavalcade of the Golden West.

Gilbert Kneiss, the Pacific Coast representative of the Railway & Locomotive Historical Society, was also assistant director of the exposition's historical drama. He was searching for suitable railroad equipment for a reenactment of the 1869 Golden Spike ceremony.

In May 1937 Kneiss traveled to Battle Mountain and explored the Nevada Central Railroad. Inside the enginehouse were two diamond stack engines, while outside he found three others, all dating back to the 1870s and 1880s. A nearby shed contained the ornate coach *Silver State*,

dusty and unused for many years, but otherwise in excellent condition. He also found the two former Monterey & Salinas Valley combines. The yards were filled with historic freight equipment in various states of disrepair.

SILVER STATE DONATED

Kneiss drove to Austin to see General Manager John Merr Hiskey. Gil Kneiss asked if Hiskey would be willing to donate the beautiful old coach to the society. Hiskey said he would take the matter up with J. G. Stokes in New York. President Stokes was agreeable, and the car was eventually given to the R&LHS.

On January 31, 1938 the Nevada Central was officially abandoned, and the last scheduled train left Austin on February 2, the day after the line's charter expired. The rails and most of the equipment were sold to the Hyman-Michaels Company of San Francisco for $17,500. Scrap-

Nevada Central locomotives and cars survived due to the efforts of historian Gilbert Kneiss, pictured (on right) with Superintendent John Hiskey. Guy Dunscomb

Many items are now displayed at the California State Railroad Museum (opposite page) in Sacramento. CSRM

ping operations began with the first rails being removed on April 20, 1938.

Gilbert Kneiss then contacted Hyman-Michaels and asked if the scrapper would be willing to donate locomotive #6 and combine #1 to the Railway & Locomotive Historical Society for restoration and use at the exposition. The dismantling firm agreed to the donation.

Kneiss had now secured a 2-6-0 locomotive (#6), a coach and combination car for the historical reenactment. Mogul #2 was used by the scrappers throughout the summer and fall of 1938.

KIMBALL BUYS #2
After the last of the old 35-pound rails had been removed on September 27, 1938, Hiskey offered to sell the two remaining locomotives, 2-6-0 #2 and 4-4-0 #5. Railfan and Disney artist Ward Kimball, with the help of Kneiss and Gerald Best, was able to purchase Mogul #2 in late 1938.

Ownership of the former North Pacific Coast 1876 Baldwin 4-4-0 was retained by Hiskey, who leased #5 to A. C. Vollmann for use at the Golden Gate Exposition in December 1938. The lease agreement placed the engine in the trust and care of the Pacific Coast Chapter (R&LHS), who was responsible for maintenance, storage and preservation. Hiskey remained the owner.

By late September, the two locomotives and two passenger cars slated for exposition use were loaded aboard standard gauge flats and gondola cars for shipment to Oakland. Here they were rebuilt, repainted and beautifully restored at the Western Pacific shops. NC's 2-6-0s #1 and #4 and metal parts from the rolling stock were also shipped off as scrap iron.

On February 18, 1939 the Cavalcade of the Golden West opened on Treasure Island. NC's 4-4-0 #5 played the role of Central Pacific *Jupiter*, and the *Silver State* was lettered as the CP's Stanford. NC's 2-6-0 #6 appeared as Union Pacific's #119, with combine #1 lettered "U.P.R.R." in the Gold Spike scene. The fact that they were narrow gauge did not seem to matter as they steamed on stage. The show was a big hit.

SECOND SEASON
The Golden Gate International Exposition's second season opened on May 25, 1940. The equipment was cleaned up at SP's West Oakland shops. The show featured a slightly different historical pageant entitled America, Cavalcade of a Nation. The *Silver State* and 4-4-0 were still lettered for the Central Pacific and Mogul #6 and combine #1 again represented the Union Pacific's train in the Wedding of the Rails. When the exposition ended in October of 1940, the equipment was moved to the West Oakland shops for storage.

After the Golden Gate International Exposition closed in 1940, the R&LHS moved the former Nevada Central locomotives and cars to various storage sites in the Bay area. They were moved to the Pacific Guano Company yards in Berkeley (1941), Moore Drydock Corporation in Oakland (1950), and the Key System Inspection Building in Oakland (1964).

With each passing year the two locomotives and pair of cars showed increased deterioration, rust and damage from vandalism. By the time the R&LHS transferred ownership to the State of California for a proposed railroad museum on March 1, 1969, locomotives #5 and #6 were little more than rusted hulks, and the two wooden passenger cars were badly rotted from many years of outside storage and exposure to the elements.

The NC equipment was moved to the Restoration Shop of the California State Railroad Museum in 1977. Over the next few years archivists and restoration specialists rebuilt the cars and locomotives for display.

NC's 4-4-0 was cosmetically reconstructed as the original 1876 North Pacific Coast #12, the *Sonoma*. Combine #1 was rebuilt as Monterey & Salinas Valley #1. The *Silver State* was also restored to its original condition.

After more than 10 years of planning and construction, the $14 million, 100,000-square-foot three-story California State Railroad Museum opened on May 2, 1981 in Old Sacramento's Historic District.

The American Standard and two cars comprise a complete train in the main exhibition hall. Mogul #6 assumed its previous identity as Nevada Short Line #1 and heads a 1920s narrow gauge freight train display on a trestle 24 feet above the main floor. The train consists of two Southern Pacific narrow gauge cars (box and tank) and a Pacific Coast Railway sidedoor caboose from Ward Kimball's Grizzly Flats Railroad collection.

Equipment from two Nevada short lines, the standard gauge Virginia & Truckee and the narrow gauge Nevada Central, provide the major historical examples of early day railroading in the American West. Safe from scrappers torches, rust and alkali dust, the NC lives.

Locomotives 5 (above) and 2 (below) occupy tracks inside the corrugated iron enginehouse addition in the late 1930s. Too beautiful to be scrapped, both were saved. Richard B. Jackson, Gilbert Kneiss

Former Nevada Central #5 (below) is dressed up as Central Pacific's *Jupiter* in 1939 at Oakland, California (above). Author's collection

Nevada Central's 1879 Mogul #6 became "Union Pacific 119" at the Golden Gate International Exposition on Treasure Island in 1939-40. Author's collection

The restored equipment of the Nevada Central played all the parts in the 1939 pageant "Cavalcade of the Golden West,"
which reenacted the driving of the Golden Spike. The CP's *Jupiter* was portrayed (this page) by NC #5. R.J. Berry, Arnold Menke
collection, Guy L. Dunscomb

NC's #6 stood in for UP's #119 (next page). Author's collection, Guy L. Dunscomb

For the Exposition's second season in 1940, the NC equipment was cleaned up (this page) at the SP's West Oakland shops. R.H. McFarland, Arnold Menke collection, author's collection

Nevada Central's combine #1 (above) and *Silver State* coach were again used for the "Wedding of the Rails" scene. *Author's collection, Guy L. Dunscomb*

RUSTING RELICS

After the close of the Exposition, the Nevada Central engines and cars were stored in the Bay area at the Pacific Guano Company (top left) in Berkeley. Gilbert Kneiss

In 1950, they were moved to the Moore Drydock Corporation (top right and below) in Oakland. Richard F. Thomas, Gordon S. Crowell

The Bay Area's fog and salt air were not kind to the historic Nevada Central locomotives and cars. Rust and rot took their toll on the equipment sitting near the water at Moore Drydock Corporation in the 1950s. Richard F. Thomas and Gordon S. Crowell

WARD KIMBALL'S GRIZZLY FLATS RAILROAD

Walt Disney animator Ward Kimball purchased #2 in late 1938 for $400. The former *Sidney Dillon* 1881 Mogul was shipped by rail to the Southern Pacific's Taylor yards in Los Angeles. It was then trucked to an orange grove in San Gabriel, where Ward and Betty Kimball were building their home. Ward's friend Richard B. Jackson paid the $200 transportation costs.

When the battered and worn old engine arrived, Ward confided that he thought he might have made "a terrible mistake." The 2-6-0 joined a former Carson & Colorado coach, for which Ward paid $50.

Ward originally planned to use the coach to house an O scale Virginia & Truckee model railroad. When they acquired the locomotive they decided to build their own backyard rail line called the Grizzly Flats Railroad.

RENAMED *EMMA NEVADA*

Following five years of part time work by Ward, Betty and many friends, #2, now renamed *Emma Nevada*, was steamed up for the first time in 1943. Walt Disney frequently visited the GFRR, and it is believed to have been the inspiration for what would later become the Disneyland Railroad.

Eventually, the tracks were lengthened along the driveway (through Betty's flower garden). A two-stall enginehouse, water tank and windmill were added. Walt Disney gave Ward the depot set from the motion picture *So Dear To My Heart*. An Hawaiian 0-4-2T was acquired in 1948, and the rebuilt sugar plantation engine was named *Chloe* after the Kimballs' daughter.

Eventually more rolling stock was added, including a Pacific Coast Ry. boxcar and caboose in 1946. These were joined by Jerry Best's *Olomana*, another Baldwin 0-4-2T from Hawaii. In 1960, the GFRR received a gondola and stock car from the SP's Owens Valley narrow gauge line. Best's 0-4-2T was given to the Smithsonian in 1977.

In September 1992, Ward and Betty, his wife of 66 years, donated the *Emma Nevada* and most of the cars to the Empire Railway Museum in Paris, California. Included was a substantial gift in order for the museum to construct a special building to house the Grizzly Flats RR collection.

...A TERRIBLE MISTAKE!

Famed Disney animator Ward Kimball (opposite top) purchased Nevada Central's #2 in 1939. Dave Gooley

When Ward first saw the battered Mogul (above and below), he confided that he might have made "a terrible mistake!" Author's collection

Ward and his wife Betty began to restore the engine and a former Carson & Colorado coach. An 1869 Union Pacific "harp" switchstand (opposite lower) was soon added to the growing collection. Richard B. Jackson

After five years of work by Ward and Betty Kimball, with the help of a number of friends, the #2 of the Grizzly Flats Railroad began to look much as she had in the 1880s. With a new boiler jacket, box headlight and brass fittings (this page), the engine was ready to be lettered in **May 1943.** Gerald M. Best, Richard B. Jackson

RESTORATION COMPLETE

Ward holds daughter Chloe as she cleans the glass on the box headlight of the restored *Emma Nevada*. The headlight's decoration was, of course, painted by Ward himself. Restoration complete, the Grizzly Flats Railroad's 2-6-0 is steamed up for a visit by the Los Angeles Live Steamers in October 1943. Richard B. Jackson

The Grizzly Flats depot (left) was a gift to Ward Kimball by Walt Disney, a frequent visitor. It had been a prop for the movie *So Dear To My Heart*. Betty Kimball

The *Emma* steams out of the GFRR enginehouse (below) with Carson & Colorado coach #5 and Pacific Coast Ry. caboose #2 in June 1946. Richard B. Jackson

EMMA NEVADA'S 100TH BIRTHDAY

Emma Nevada was 100 years old when steamed up near the windmill-powered water tank (above) in April 1981. Ward Kimball

California State
RAILROAD
MUSEUM

The entire passenger train on the main floor of the California State Railroad Museum (opposite page) is made of beautifully restored former Nevada Central equipment. CSRM

The attention to detail is reflected (above and below) on North Pacific Coast's *Sonoma*, the former NC #5. Author's photographs

Former Nevada Central 4-4-0 #5 is displayed (above) as NPC #12, the *Sonoma* of 1876. CSRM

Nevada Central's combine #1 was rebuilt and lettered for the Monterey & Salinas Valley (below), her original owner. Author's photograph

Following rebuilding and restoration, the Nevada Central's combine #1 (above) and coach *Silver State* arrive at the California State Railroad Museum in Sacramento. CSRM

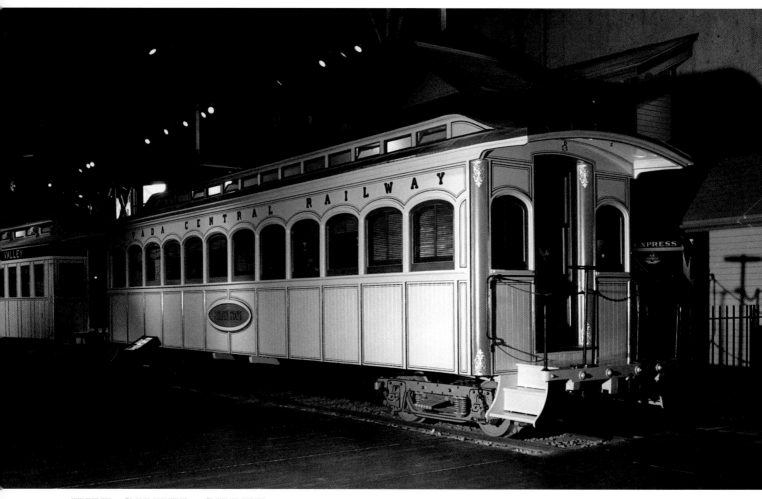

THE SILVER STATE

Resplendent in original mustard-yellow paint, the *Silver State* was restored to its 1880s appearance for display on the CSRM's main exhibition floor, complete with ornate paint and striping inside and out. Years of careful research and attention to detail by the museum's staff resulted in a beautiful reconstruction of the car that was built in the Nevada Central's Battle Mountain shop.
Author's photographs

A MUCH TRAVELED MOGUL

Nevada Central's #6 was a true narrow gauge "boomer." It was built by Baldwin in 1879 for the Utah & Northern and served on the Oregon Short Line & Utah Northern (UP), the Golconda & Adelaide RR and Nevada Short Line Ry. before coming to the NC in 1922. The 2-6-0 saw only a few years of use on the NC and was out of regular service by late 1927. Yet, it survived the scrappers. It arrived from the restoration shop (below) as NSL #1 and is displayed with a freight train on a wooden trestle (left), high above the main floor of the museum. CSRM, author's photograph

CHAPTER 13
NUTS & BOLTS

Equipment & Plans

THROUGHOUT ITS LIFETIME, the Nevada Central Railroad owned only eight locomotives, all but two of which were second, third or fourthhand. After some 50 years of research and with the help of several knowledgeable historians, a comprehensive locomotive roster has been compiled.

The car roster is another matter, as those records have not survived. Like the locomotives, the cars came from a number of different sources, and few were actually built for the Sagebrush Narrow Gauge.

An 1898 listing of each car, its capacity and condition is by far the most accurate and detailed rolling stock roster and is presented with additional notes gleaned from many different sources. Many of the cars on this list were still on the property at the time of abandonment in 1938.

Poor's Manual listings of NC equipment over the years 1880s-1930s provide some information about the rolling stock, but essentially reflect total numbers, a decrease in "platform cars" (flats) and a corresponding increase in coal and stock cars.

The Battle Mountain newspaper often reported the arrival of equipment but seldom specified what type or the source. The problem is compounded by a report that many of the early records were disposed of by being dropped down an abandoned mine shaft near the Stokes' Castle in Austin.

AUSTIN IS SECURED
In October 1879 the NC received 20 new flat cars and 10 box cars from the Eastern carbuilder Billmeyer & Small of York, Pennsylvania. Ten "rubble cars" (flats) and Mason Bogie #2, the *Austin*, then arrived from the nearby Eureka & Palisade.

A month later the NC began receiving 40 flats, eight box, two "iron" cars and two combines from the Monterey & Salinas Valley. These were the first cars constructed by the famed Carter Brothers firm.

The NC purchased rail and several cars from the still-born Stockton & Ione RR. They included three box cars, a combination (passenger-caboose) and a passenger car frame. They are believed to have been built by the Holt Brothers in Stockton. The S&I box cars were of very light construction and were set aside as lineside structures at Bobtown, Dillon and Watts in the 1890s. Half of one of these cars still exists near Berlin, Nevada at the Ichthyosaur State Park.

The former Monterery & Salinas Valley Baldwin 2-6-0 arrived in December 1897, becoming NC's #3, the *Anson P. Stokes*. In January 1880, the M&SV 4-4-0 became #4, the *Daniel B. Hatch*. Also arriving was former North Pacific Coast 4-4-0 *Sonoma*, named the *Gen'l J.H. Ledlie*.

A "caboose" was sold to the Utah Eastern along with 10 flats and locomotives (1st) #1 and #3 on October 30, 1880. Newspaper articles refer to the 4-wheel crummy as "the black caboose," and it is believed to have been the former S&I car. The equipment was shipped in December 1880, soon after the NC was completed.

OMAHA SHOPS
Following the Union Pacific's June 1881 acquisition (Chapter 5), the *Railway Gazette* reported on September 16, 1881 that the UP's Omaha Shops were building "20 box (sic) cars" for the NC. These cars were actually 10-ton "taper-sill" flat cars. Some of these 27-foot-long flats were rebuilt as coal (gondola), stock cars and box cars, retaining the car numbers regardless of car type.

After 1882, the NC's rolling stock roster saw few additions. Two Nevada Short Line flats (#27-28) were purchased in 1920. The NSL obtained these flats from the Nevada-California-Oregon in 1917. The NC rebuilt them into high-side coal cars, retaining their old numbers. Two side-door gondolas (#301-302) were obtained in trade with the Eureka-Nevada Ry. (former E&P) for Motor #105 in 1931. These gons were built by J. Hammond's California Car Works (1904) for the Tonopah RR and went to the E&P in 1907.

Five tank cars owned by the Standard Oil Company operated over the NC and carried numbers X-50, X-100, X-104, X-105 and X-189.

Accidents and rebuildings may account for some changes, however, the 1898 Roster provides a good basis for reconstructing an accurate listing.

NEVADA CENTRAL
LOCOMOTIVE ROSTER

Number	Type	Builder	C/N-Date	Cylinders	Drivers
1	2-6-0	Brooks	230-9/1875	11 x 16	35-3/4"

Original Bath & Hammondsport RR #2 *Jonathan Robie*
Nevada Central #1 *Battle Mountain* (9/1879)
Utah Eastern #1 (12/1880)
Echo & Park City #1 (1887)

Number	Type	Builder	C/N-Date	Cylinders	Drivers
1(2nd)	2-6-0	Baldwin	5569-4/1881	13 x 18	41"

New for Nevada Central #1
Named *S.H.H. Clark* (UP Gen'l Supt.) after arrival (6/1881)
Out of service (12/11/1923). Supplying parts for (2nd) #2
Scrapped 1938

Number	Type	Builder	C/N-Date	Cylinders	Drivers
2	0-4-4	Mason	461-7/1872	10 x 15	33"

Mason's first "Bogie" built on speculation (1871)
Originally named *Onward*, Wt. 14 tons
Sold to American Fork Railway (4/1872). Proved too light.
Stored at Sandy, UT (c. 1873-1874)
To Eureka & Palisade RR #1 (1874)
To Nevada Central RR #2 *Austin* (10/1879) Called *The Dinky*
Renumbered (2nd) #3 (8/1881) to make room for the new (2nd) #2.
To Union Pacific for Utah & Northern (12/1882)
Rebuilt by Omaha Shops as 0-4-2T before 1885.
Utah & Northern #45 (1/1883), #296 (1885), out of service (1886)
Scrapped (1887)
Note: This may be the "Dinky" reported as switch engine on Denver, South Park & Pacific at Buena Vista, CO (1883)

Number	Type	Builder	C/N-Date	Cylinders	Drivers
2(2nd)	2-6-0	Baldwin	5575-4/1881	13 x18	41"

New for Nevada Central #2
Named *Sidney Dillon* (UP President) after arrival (6/1881)
Ward Kimball Grizzly Flats RR, San Gabriel, CA (10/1938)
Orange Empire Railway Museum, Paris, CA (9/1992) display

Number	Type	Builder	C/N-Date	Cylinders	Drivers
3	2-6-0	Baldwin	3625-7/1874	12 x 16	40"

Monterey & Salinas Valley RR #1 *C.S. Abbott* 18 tons
Nevada Central #3 *Anson P. Stokes* arrived (12/27/1879)
Utah Eastern RR #3 *General Burton* (10/1880)
Lettered *Robt. S. Walker* before shipment to UE (12/1880)
Renumbered Utah Eastern (UP Syst.) #289 (1885)
Kilpatrick Brothers & Collins, contractors (1894)
Cincinnati, Georgetown & Portsmouth #3 *Sally*
Cincinnati Equipment Co., Ohio dealer (1903-1905)
Laurel Ry. (T.W. Thayer Lumber Co.) #3 *Damascus*, VA (c.1905)

Number	Type	Builder	C/N-Date	Cylinders	Drivers
4	4-4-0	Baldwin	3682-1/1875	13 x 18	42"

New for Monterey & Salinas Valley RR #2 *Monterey*
Nevada Central #4 *D.B. Hatch* arrived (1/16/1880)
First NC use on construction train (1/23/1880)
Out of service for repairs (2/1898); probably not repaired
At Battle Mountain shops (derelict) until scrapped (1938)

| 5 | 4-4-0 | Baldwin | 3843-3/1876 | 12 x 16 | 42" |

New for North Pacific Coast #12 *Sonoma*
Nevada Central #5 *Gen'l J.H. Ledlie* arrived (1/1880)
First NC use (1/26/1880) overhauled (10/6/1880)
Renamed *Jos. Collett* NC's General Manager (10/1880)
Operational until NC shut down (1938)
Owned by J.M. Hiskey, leased to Golden Gate Exposition under care of Pacific Coast
Chapter R&LHS (1938-1969)
Ownership transferred to State of California (3/1/1969)
California State Railroad Museum, Sacramento, CA (1977)
Deeded to State by Hiskey heirs (1978)
On display: CSRM as North Pacific Coast #12 *Sonoma*

| 6 | 2-6-0 | Baldwin | 4562-3/1879 | 12 x 18 | 40" |

New for Utah & Northern Ry. #13, U&N/OSL&UN (UP) #17 (1885)
Golconda & Adelaide RR #1 *Pearl* (10/1898)
Sugarman Iron & Metal Co. (1913)
Nevada Short Line Ry #1 (1914)
Western Machinery Co. for sale in *Railway Age* advertisement (7/1920)
Nevada Central #6 (1922)
Out of service (10/8/1927)
Hyman-Michaels Co. (1938)
Pacific Coast Chapter R&LHS (1938)
Golden Gate Int'l Exposition, Treasure Island (1938-1939)
Ownership transferred to State of California (3/1/1969)
California State Railroad Museum, Sacramento, CA (1977)
On display: CSRM as Nevada Short Line #1 (1981)

Thanks to Cornelius W. Hauck, Garrie L. Tufford, Kyle K. Wyatt and Gregory Maxwell for their assistance.

Nevada Central's 2-6-0 #3 (Baldwin 1874), the *Anson P. Stokes*, managed to escape being photographed on the NC, having been sold in 1880 to the Utah Eastern. The only known photo shows her on the Laurel Railway, in Virginia, in about 1911. Cornelius W. Hauck collection

Nevada Central's (2nd) #1 the *S.H.H. Clark* (top) was out of service by late 1923, but supplied parts to sister #2. Gilbert Kneiss

Mogul (2nd) #2 had a long career on the Sagebrush Narrow Gauge and was used (right) to dismantle the tracks in 1938. Richard B. Jackson

Number 4 *D.B. Hatch* was built by Baldwin in 1875 for the Monterey & Salinas Valley. The 4-4-0 sat for many years (below) near the Battle Mountain shops and was finally scrapped in 1938. Richard B. Jackson

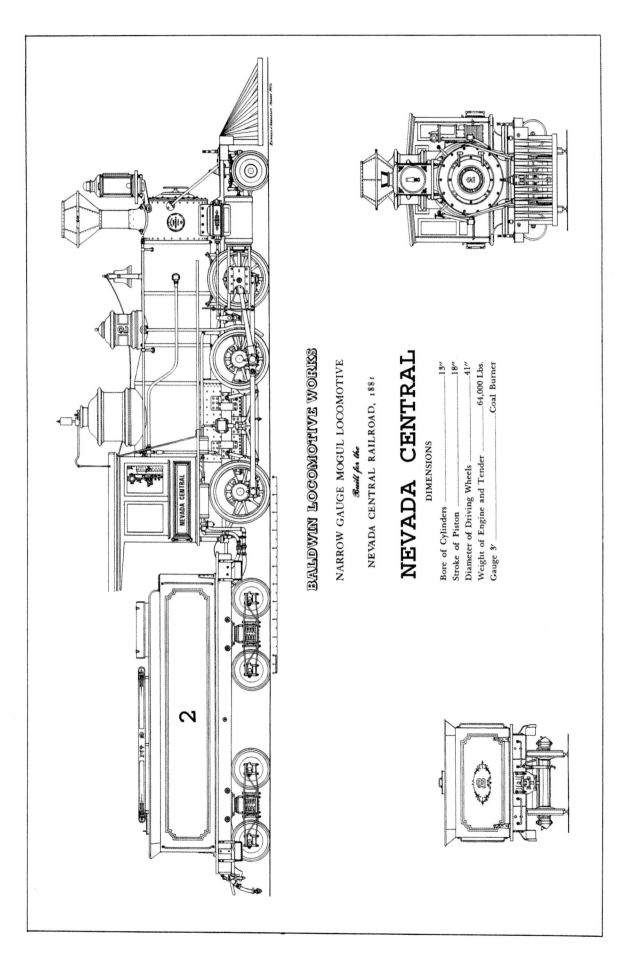

BALDWIN LOCOMOTIVE WORKS

NARROW GAUGE MOGUL LOCOMOTIVE

Built for the

NEVADA CENTRAL RAILROAD, 1881

NEVADA CENTRAL

DIMENSIONS

Bore of Cylinders	13"
Stroke of Piston	18"
Diameter of Driving Wheels	41"
Weight of Engine and Tender	64,000 Lbs.
Gauge 3'	Coal Burner

Nevada Central's second #2 served the road for many years and lasted long enough to be preserved by Ward Kimball. Built by Baldwin in 1881, it is now at the Orange Empire Railway Museum in Southern California. *Drawing by Edward J. Sargean*

THE FIVE SPOT

The Nevada Central's 4-4-0 #5, the
Gen'l J.H. Ledlie, was built by Baldwin
for the North Pacific Coast in 1876,
but spent most of its life on the NC. It
carries an iron snowplow pilot (above)
at Clifton in the early 1900s. J.M.
Hiskey, author's collection

The #5 sits in the metal enginehouse
addition (below) and in the yards
(right) at Battle Mountain in 1938.
Gilbert Kneiss, D.S. Richter

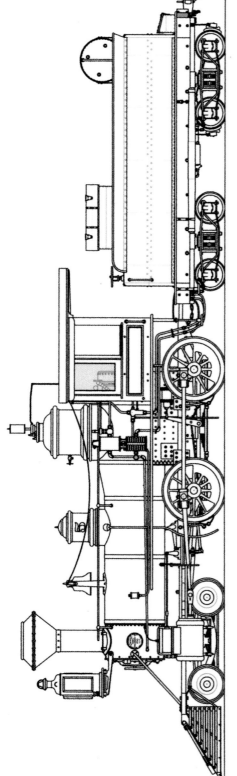

LEFT SIDE VIEW

NEVADA CENTRAL R. R.
ENGINE NO. 5
ca. 1899 - 1902

DRAWN BY ROBERT D. BAILEY

SCALE 0 1 2 3 4 5 6

REAR VIEW

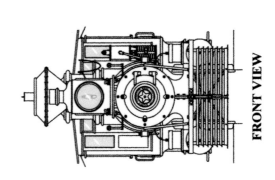

BALDWIN LOCOMOTIVE WORKS
BURNHAM, PARRY,
WILLIAMS&Cᵒ
Nᵒ3843
1876
PHILADELPHIA

FRONT VIEW

NARROW GAUGE BOOMER

In railroading parlance, a "boomer" was a man who drifted from one rail line to another. Nevada Central's Mogul #6 was a true boomer, having served on many different roads. It first served the Utah & Northern as #13 (above) and came to the NC from the Nevada Short Line (below), where it was #1. Author's collection, Bert H. Ward

The #6 sat out of service in the Battle Mountain yards (bottom) for many years. Richard B. Jackson

It was shipped to Oakland (left) and rebuilt as U.P. #119 for the Golden Gate Exposition (below) in 1939. Richard B. Jackson, Harold K. Vollrath collection

The early Utah & Northern pass is from the author's collection.

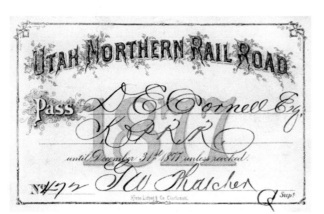

THE NEVADA CENTRAL RAILROAD COMPANY
INVENTORY OF STOCK AT BATTLE MOUNTAIN FEBRUARY 28, 1898

Number	Remarks
Engine #1 (2nd)	First class condition
Engine #2 (2nd)	Needs new firebox
Engine #4	Will take about $1,000 worth of material to put her in running order, needs new flues, new tires, half door sheet, set of brasses for rods and drivers, new engine truck wheels, axles and springs, lubricator, injectors, lagging jacket and steam gauge.
Engine #5	Running order, needs new flues, cylinder bored, new pistons, drivin (sic) tires turned and light overhauling.
Saddle Tank Motor (*Mules' Relief*)	needs injector, pump, steam gauge, flues resetting, flue sheet chipped and caulked, otherwise condition good, cost about $150 to repair.
Motor	Running order (*Go Devil*).
Coach #1	Good running order (combination car)
Coach #2	First class condition, good as new (combine car)
Coach #3	First class condition (*Silver State*)
Caboose #1	Needs four new wheels, new roof and part of one side, doors and windows. Cost about $75 to put in running order.

Number			Remarks		
#50 Stock	10 tons capacity,		good running order		(Note 1)
#51 Stock	"	"	"		"
#52 Stock	"	"	"		"
#53 Flat	"	"	"		"
#54 Stock	"	"	"		"
#55 Coal	"	"	"		"
#56 Coal	"	"	"		"
#57 Stock	"	"	"		"
#58 Flat	"	"	"		"
#59 Flat	"	"	"		"
#60 Flat	"	"	"		"
#61 Coal	"	"	"		"
#62 Flat	"	"	"		"
#63 Flat	"	"	complete wreck		"
#64 Coal	"	"	good running order		"
#65 Stock	"	"	"		"
#66 Coal	"	"	"		"
#67 Coal	"	"	"		"
#68 Flat	"	"	"		"
#69 Flat	"	"	"		"
#100 Flat	8 tons capacity,		good running order		(Note 2)
#101 Flat	"	"	"		"
#102 Flat	"	"	needs new wheels, brake beams		"
#104 Coal	"	"	good running order		"
#105 Flat	"	"	needs new deck, brake beams		"
#108 Coal	"	"	good running order		"
#109 Flat	"	"	needs new deck and wheels		"
#110 Flat	"	"	good running order		"
#111 Flat	"	"	"		"
#112 Flat	"	"	frame good shape, needs new deck and wheels		"
#113 Coal	"	"	good running order		"

Car			Condition	Note
#115 Flat	"	"	only frame left, needs new deck and two trucks	"
#116 Flat	"	"	good running order	"
#118 Flat	"	"	complete wreck	"
#152 Flat	"	"	frame good, needs half new deck, one axle and 8 wheels	(Note 3)
#154 Flat	"	"	good running order (later rebuilt as open top stock car)	"
#155 Flat	"	"	needs new set of wheels	"
#156 Flat	"	"	good running order	"
#157 Flat	"	"	"	"
#158 Flat	"	"	"	"
#159 Flat	"	"	"	"
#160 Flat	"	"	needs 8 new wheels and small amount of repairs on deck	"
#161 Flat	"	"	needs new wheels, two axles	"
#162 Flat	"	"	needs new wheels, axles, deck	"
#163 Flat	"	"	good running order	"
#164 Flat	"	"	"	"
#165 Flat	"	"	needs 1 new side sill, two complete trucks and brake rigging	"
#166 Flat	"	"	good running order	"
#167 Flat	"	"	needs 4 new wheels and one complete truck	"
#168 Flat	"	"	needs new wheels, otherwise good	"
#169 Flat	"	"	good running order	"
#170 Flat	"	"	"	"
#172 Flat	"	"	"	"
#200 Box	"	"	needs new floor and doors	(Note 4)
#201 Box	"	"	good running order	"
#202 Box	"	"	"	"
#203 Box	"	"	"	"
#204 Box	"	"	"	"
#205 Box	"	"	(became cook car 1917)	"
#206 Box	"	"	good running order	"
#207 Box	"	"	"	"
#208 Box	"	"	"	"
#209 Box	"	"	"	"
#252 Box	"	"	"	(Note 5)
#253 Box	"	"	"	"
#254 Box	"	"	"	"
#255 Box	"	"	"	"
#256 Box	"	"	"	"

NOTES

Note 1: Twenty flats #50-69 (27' long, 10-ton, taper-sill) built by Union Pacific's Omaha Shops in 1881. Some converted to coal, stock and (later) box cars. In 3/1895 the NC rebuilt four flats as stock cars, adding one more in early 1898. In 1901 some Billmeyer & Small flats reported rebuilt as stock cars. In October, 1925 the NC had 10 stock cars #50-54, 57, 64-67. Other flats later converted to stock cars included 60, 154.

Note 2: Twenty flats #100-119 (8 ton) built by Billmeyer & Small, York, PA (10/1879).

Note 3: Last of 40 Monterey & Salinas Valley (24', 8 tons) flats built by Carter Brothers in 1874 as M&SV #1-79 (odd numbers). Sold to the NC in 1879. Ten flats sold to the Utah Eastern in 1880 may have included some of these cars.

Note 4: Ten box cars (#200-209) built new by Billmeyer & Small, York, PA in October 1879.

Note 5: Last of 8 original M&SV (24', 8 ton) box cars built by Carter Brothers in 1874 as M&SV #2-16 (even numbers).

Additonal Notes: Three box cars came from the Stockton & Ione (c.1879-80). S&I cars believed to have been built by Holt Brothers, Stockton, CA (1876) and were of very light construction. Off roster by February 1898. Cars became lineside structures at Bobtown, Dillon and Watts in 1890s. Half of the Bobtown car exists at Ichthyosaur State Park near Berlin, NV.

Two flat cars purchased from Nevada Short Line (#27-28) in 1921. Converted to high side coal cars by Battle Mountain Shop (4/1921), retaining their NSL numbers. They were acquired by the NSL from the Nevada-California-Oregon in 1917.

Two side-door gondolas acquired in trade with Eureka Nevada Ry. (#301-302) in 1931 for NC Motor 105.

Five Standard Oil Co. tank cars operated on the NC:
S.O.CO. X-100 former Lake Tahoe Ry. & Trans., to NC 9/1925. Car wrecked 1927, tank placed on former stock car #50.
NC   X-50   former stock car #50 with tank from X-100. Retired 1/1938 and tank used at Austin bulk plant.
S.O.CO. X-104 built by N-C-O in 1915 as A-6. To S.O.CO. in 1927 ($400) and shipped to NC (1928). To NCNG in 1938.
S.O.CO. X-105 built by N-C-O as A-7. To S.O.CO. in 1927 and shipped to NC in 1927. To NCNG in 1938.
S.O.CO. X-189 built by NCNG in 1916 as #67. To S.O.CO. and shipped to NC as X-189 in 1934. Retired 1/1938 and tank to Battle Mountain bulk plant.

A ROLLING MUSEUM

By the late 1930's the "rip tracks" at Battle Mountain were filled with antique rolling stock, some dating back to the 1870's. Bob Brown collection, Ted Wurm

A row of eclectic cars (top) fill a siding at Battle Mountain at the end of operations. They include (left to right) box 208, flat 100, box 206, flat 154, a high-side gondola, home-built box and stock cars. Ed Bond collection

The shop area (bottom) contained more pieces of ancient rolling stock, most of which were burned for their scrap metal. Gilbert Kneiss

The pair of Nevada Central combines were the first passenger cars built by the Carter Brothers in 1874 for the Monterey & Salinas Valley, Califiornia's first narrow gauge. Both were on the line at the end of operations in 1938. Combine #1 (above) was preserved, while #2 was scrapped. Gerald M. Best, Linwood Moody collection

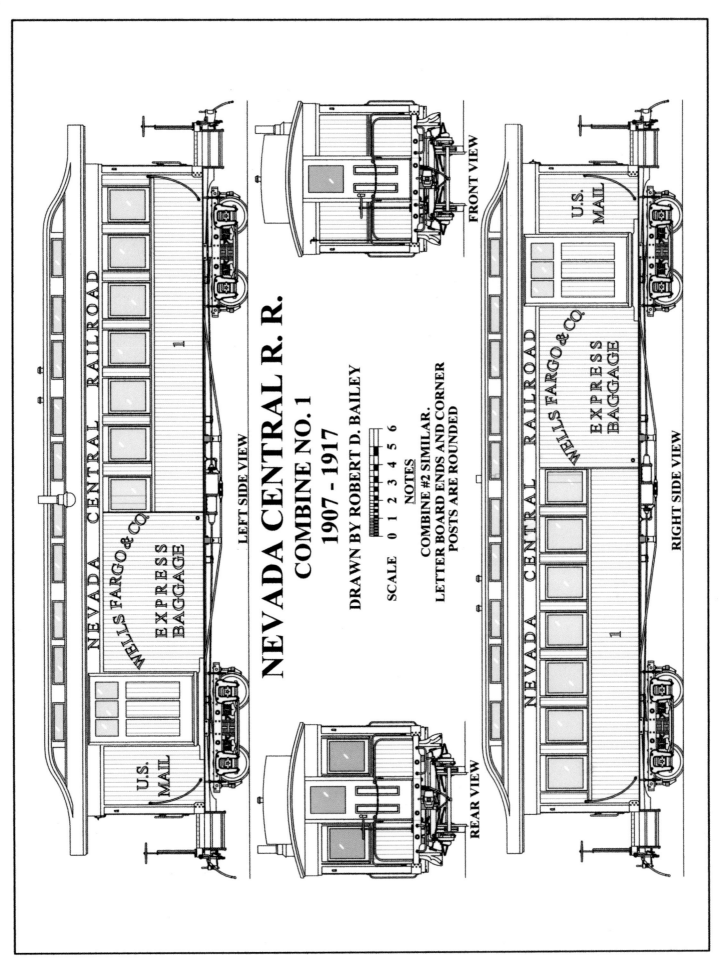

NEVADA CENTRAL R. R.

COMBINE NO. 1
1907 – 1917

DRAWN BY ROBERT D. BAILEY

SCALE 0 1 2 3 4 5 6

NOTES

COMBINE #2 SIMILAR.
LETTER BOARD ENDS AND CORNER
POSTS ARE ROUNDED

LEFT SIDE VIEW

RIGHT SIDE VIEW

FRONT VIEW

REAR VIEW

NEVADA CENTRAL EQUIPMENT COLORS

COMBINATION CARS 1 AND 2

1874   Built by Carter Brothers as Monterey & Salinas Valley #1, #2. Painted yellow with mahogany letter-board and trim. Repainted with same colors in November 1875.

1879   To Nevada Central RR, kept same colors, except letterboard painted dark brown with new gold/yellow lettering. Cars varnished.

1882   Repainted mustard yellow in September. Letterboard changed from "Railroad" to "Railway" (during UP era). Newspaper article states color was "buff."

1886   Rebuilt from 9 to 7 windows. Retained yellow/buff paint.

1889   Baggage section enlarged and lettering changed back to "Railroad" after UP control ended in November 1888.

1895   Painted dark brown in July.

1901   Westinghouse air brakes installed.

1902   Janney (3/4 size) automatic couplers installed.

1907   "Wells, Fargo & Company" lettering added.

1927   Painted dark green, brown letterboard, gold/yellow letters.

SILVER STATE (COACH #3)

1880-81   Built by Battle Mountain Shops. Painted mustard yellow.

1887   Repainted "creamy yellow." News reports say "yellow/tan."

1895   Painted black with red trim.

1900   Painted dark red/brown.

1901   Westinghouse air brakes added.

1902   Janney (3/4 size) automatic couplers installed.

1906-16   Reportedly painted steel gray and brown.

NOTE: Passenger cars seldom used after motor cars took over daily schedules (1913). Combine #1 damaged in Coach House fire (1927) and had only half of car body painted green in 1938. Combine #1 and *Silver State* to Railway & Locomotive Historical Society (1939).

FREIGHT EQUIPMENT
FLAT & BOX CARS

1881   All box and flat cars painted yellow.

1897   Cars repainted boxcar red. (i.e. dark red brown)

1938   Most cars lacked any paint.

STOCK CARS

Stock cars rebuilt from flatcars by NC Car Shops, with corresponding decrease in flat cars, when cattle and sheep shipments began to exceed mining related traffic after 1890. Stock cars retained old flat car numbers.

1895   Master Mechanic J.C. Slater completed four "new" stock cars in March.

1898   NC Shops converted more flats to stock cars in June

1905   Roster shows 14 stock cars.

1915   One new stock car built. May have replaced one wrecked.

CABOOSES

The "black caboose" is believed to have been the former Stockton & Ione RR combination car obtained in 1879. It was sold as a caboose to the Utah Eastern RR in 1880. Four-wheel "red caboose" #1 was built in the NC Shops in December 1880. Number 10, an eight-wheel caboose, was built by the NC in 1913. Later used as a bunk car and on line at end of operations.

WORK CARS

1891   A new wedge snowplow was completed by Boilermaker James Perkins in February. Brown frame with black (iron) plow.

1892   A new pile driver was built on a flat car for use in repairing bridges and trestles due to frequent washouts.

SILVER STATE

Pride of the Nevada Central was the coach *Silver State*, built in the company shops in 1880-81. Seldom used in later years, the ornate car was loaded aboard a standard gauge flat (above and right) and taken to Oakland in 1938. R.H. McFarland, Arnold Menke collection, Gerald M. Best

Rebuilt for the Golden Gate Exposition (below), the car was lettered as Central Pacific's *Stanford*. R.H. McFarland, Arnold Menke collection

BOX CAR #204

Ancient Nevada Central box #204 was still in service at
the end of operations. The 24-foot-long, 8-ton capacity car
sported single spring trucks and had riveted truss rods, not
turnbuckles. Dick Jackson (above) and Ted Wurm (below)
found it at Battle Mountain in June of 1938.

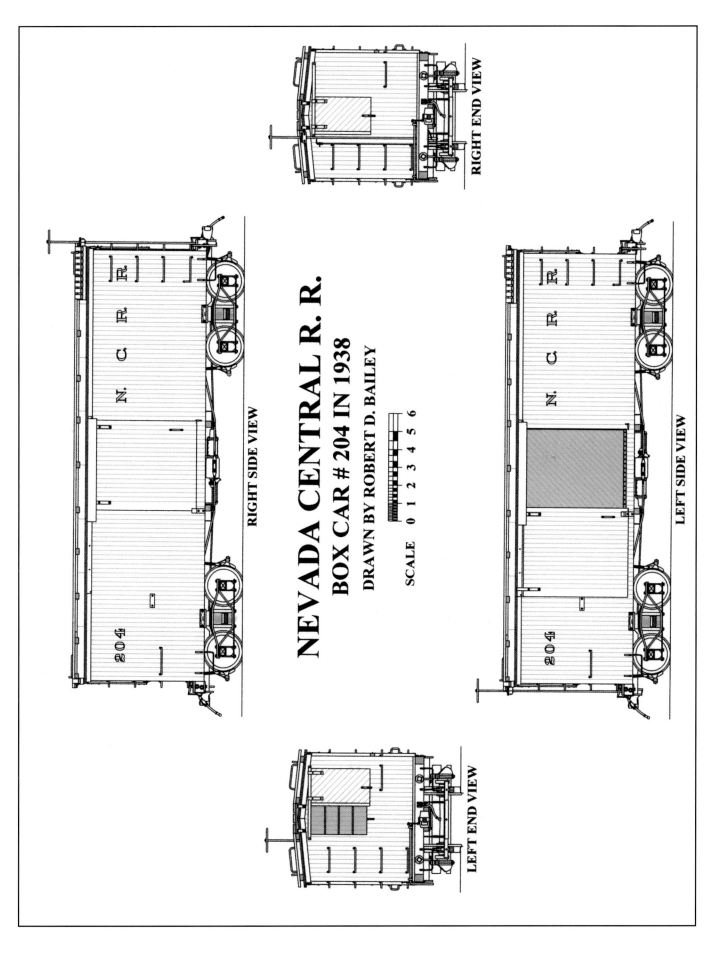

RIGHT END VIEW

NEVADA CENTRAL R. R.
BOX CAR # 204 IN 1938
DRAWN BY ROBERT D. BAILEY

SCALE   0 1 2 3 4 5 6

RIGHT SIDE VIEW

LEFT SIDE VIEW

LEFT END VIEW

A GALLERY OF ROLLING STOCK

Each Nevada Central car seemed to be unique. After years of service, wrecks, rebuildings, wear and tear, no two cars were alike. The variety of rolling stock is pictured on these pages. Drop side gondola #301 (opposite top) and sister #302 came in trade for a motor car from the Eureka-Nevada in 1931. The tank cars were owned by Standard Oil and some later went to the Nevada County Narrow Gauge. Linwood Moody, Grahame Hardy, Ed Bond, R.B. Jackson and Rich Dunn collections

The Nevada Central's car shop often converted existing flat cars into stock cars, gondolas and box cars. Stock car #154 (top) was a weathered gray color when found by Ted Wurm in 1938. Carter-built box #253 and gondola #56 are pictured below. The "taper sill" coal car is a converted flat. Linwood Moody collection

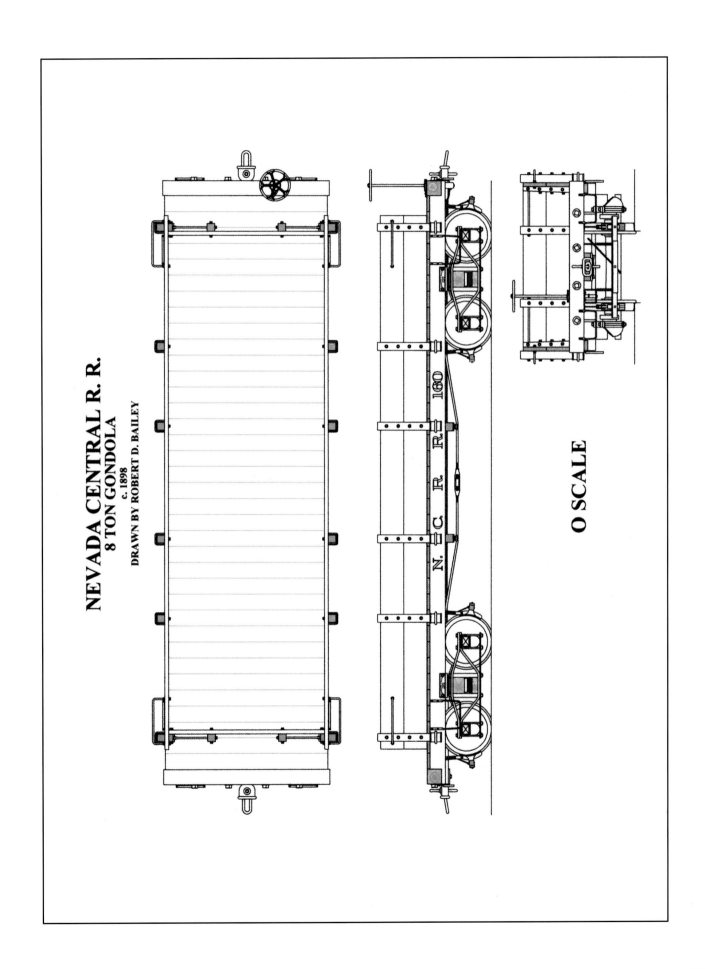

NEVADA CENTRAL R. R.
8 TON GONDOLA
c. 1898
DRAWN BY ROBERT D. BAILEY

N. C. R. R. 160

O SCALE

A UNIQUE RELIC

Nevada Central's box #253 is a rare first generation Carter Brothers car, built in 1874. The 8-ton capacity car had swing bolster trucks and was 24' long. The car was still in service during 1938 scrapping operations and is preserved today at Ardenwood Park, near Fremont, California. Richard B. Jackson

Boxcar #253 is unique in several ways. It was built by Carter Brothers for the Monterey & Salinas Valley RR in 1874 at a cost of $575. The car came to the NC in 1880 as part of a group of eight M&SV high cars (2-16 even numbers) and 40 flats (1-79 odd numbers).

The car is 24' long, weighed about 4 tons empty, had an 8-ton capacity and was equipped with link and pin couplers. Numbered 253 on the NC, it received Westinghouse air brakes and three-quarter-size Janney (automatic) couplers soon after 1900.

The #253 was one of five remaining former M&SV boxcars on the 1898 inventory and was in "good running order." Rebuilt in 1922-23, the car was still in service when the NC was scrapped in 1939.

Number 253 was of unusually light construction with only four sills and a single perline (roof ridge pole). After abandonment, the car body was set aside, less trucks, and when discovered by the late collector Robert Caudill, known as "Dobie Doc," it contained the complete files of the *Reese River Reveille* dating back to 1863.

The #253 was displayed with other equipment at Dobie's Last Frontier Hotel & Casino in Las Vegas. The car was moved to the Gold Strike Inn near Boulder City, Nevada in 1960. In 1992 the Society for the Preservation of Carter Resources (SPCRR) acquired #254 and moved it to Ardenwood Park, near Fremont, California. Today it is the last piece of original M&SV and NC freight equipment known to exist.

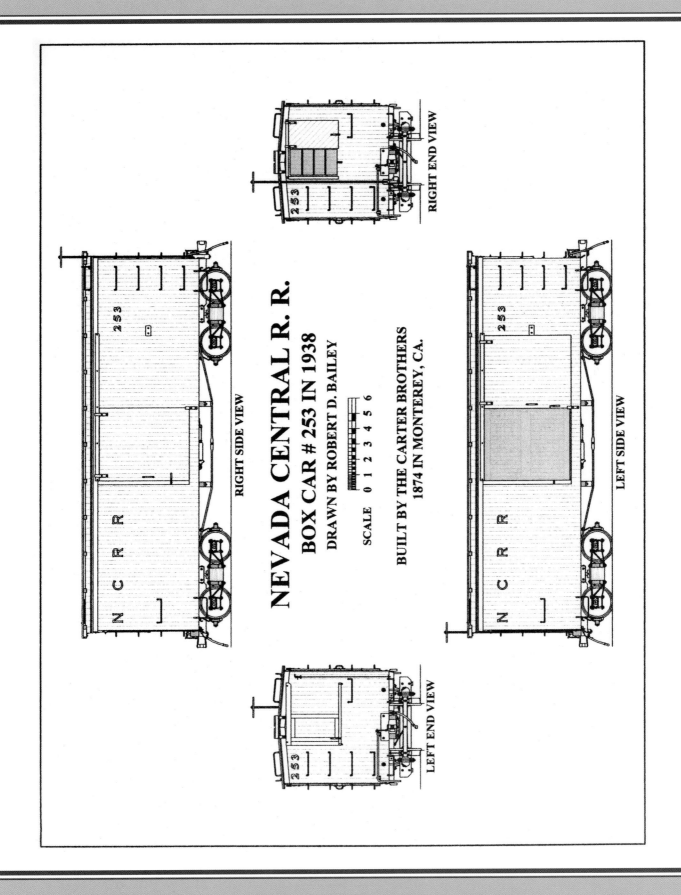

NEVADA CENTRAL R. R.
BOX CAR # 253 IN 1938
DRAWN BY ROBERT D. BAILEY

SCALE 0 1 2 3 4 5 6

BUILT BY THE CARTER BROTHERS
1874 IN MONTEREY, CA.

RIGHT SIDE VIEW

LEFT SIDE VIEW

RIGHT END VIEW

LEFT END VIEW

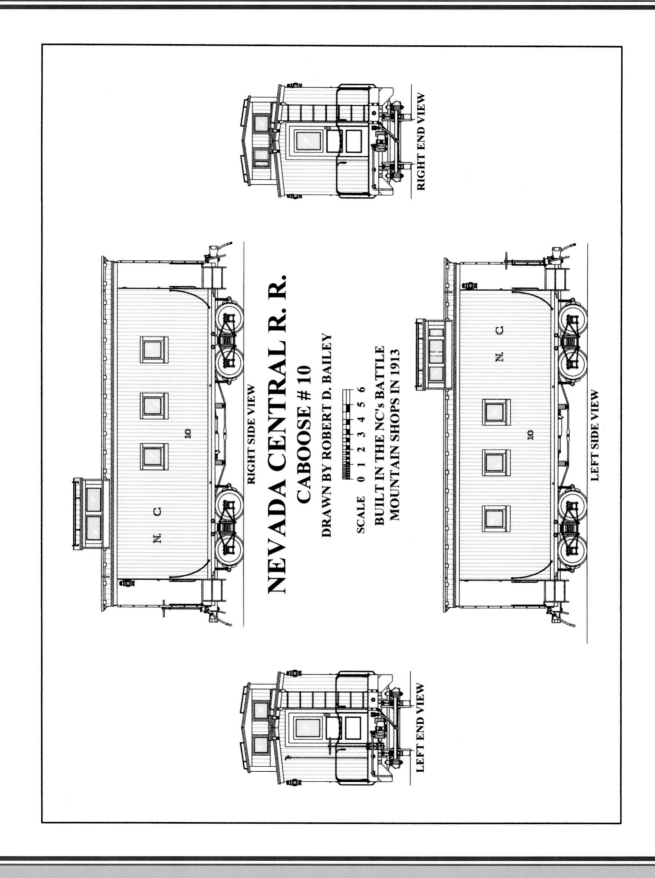

RIGHT END VIEW

RIGHT SIDE VIEW

NEVADA CENTRAL R. R.
CABOOSE # 10
DRAWN BY ROBERT D. BAILEY

SCALE 0 1 2 3 4 5 6

BUILT IN THE NC's BATTLE
MOUNTAIN SHOPS IN 1913

N. C

10

LEFT SIDE VIEW

LEFT END VIEW

CABOOSE CARS

An 8-wheel caboose was built in the NC's Battle Mountain Shops in 1913, using hardware, trucks, brake gear, etc. from an existing freight car. The "single-spring" trucks appear to have come from one of the 20 taper-sill flat cars built for the NC by UP's Omaha Shops in 1881. The cast journal box covers are of the "lift-out" style found on other UP-controlled narrow gauge roads like the Utah Northern and Colorado Central, with a pattern marked "N.G.No.1."

The 1916 ICC valuation states the car had "a wood body and underframe, 20,000-pound capacity, cupola and platforms." Condition at that time was listed, less depreciation, at $513. On October 11, 1925, the car was listed under work cars as a bunk-car-caboose #10.

The #10 had unique riveted trussrods, typical of many other NC cars, and also found on some early UN cars. A list of cars on August 14, 1937 shows it was still on hand at the end of operations.

Number 10 was the last of three NC cabooses. The first, known as the "black caboose," was sold along with two locomotives (#1, #3) and 10 flats to the Utah & Eastern RR in late 1880. This car is believed to have been the "combination" obtained in 1879 from the ill-fated Stockton & Ione.

On December 4, 1880 the *Messenger* reported, "A neat and substantial caboose has been turned out of the NC Shop. It is fitted up with seats, closets, etc." This 4-wheel caboose was painted red, and the paper noted it was "an offspring of the old black caboose, but could be seen (for) 40 miles."

Caboose #10 was built in 1913, using parts from an earlier car. The car has single spring trucks with Union Pacific-style cast journal box covers and riveted truss rods. C.W. Witbeck, Arnold Menke collections

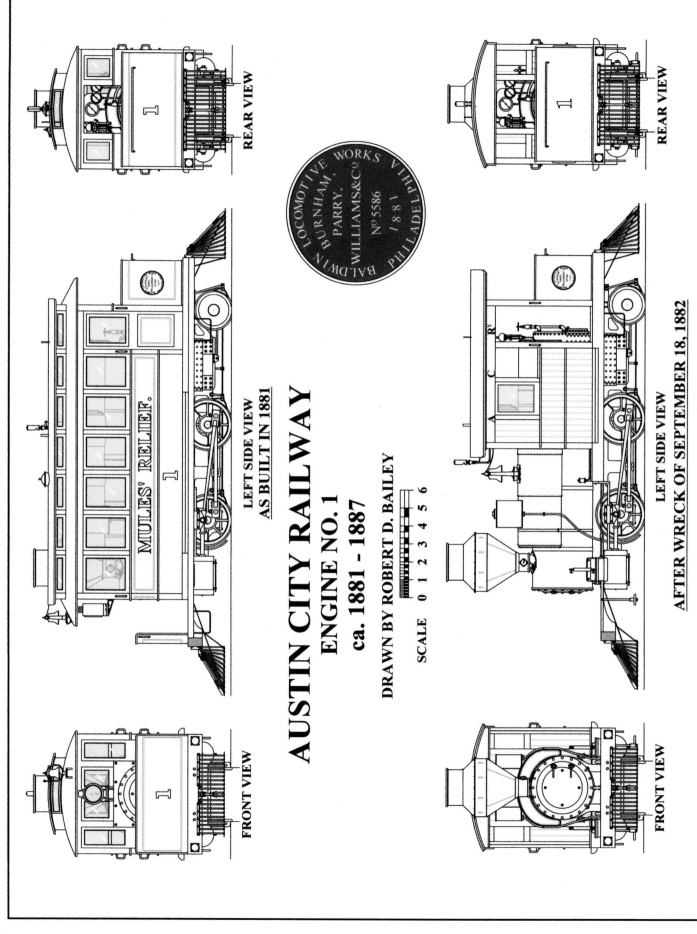

REAR VIEW

REAR VIEW

LEFT SIDE VIEW
AS BUILT IN 1881

LEFT SIDE VIEW
AFTER WRECK OF SEPTEMBER 18, 1882

MULES' RELIEF.

1

BALDWIN LOCOMOTIVE WORKS
BURNHAM. PARRY. WILLIAMS&Cᵒ
PHILADELPHIA
Nᵒ 5586
1881

AUSTIN CITY RAILWAY
ENGINE NO. 1
ca. 1881 - 1887

DRAWN BY ROBERT D. BAILEY

SCALE 0 1 2 3 4 5 6

FRONT VIEW

FRONT VIEW

BATTLE MOUNTAIN & LEWIS 1881(C)1890

NO	TYPE	BUILDER	C/N	DATE	NAME	NOTES
1	2-4-0T	Union Iron	23	1881	*John D. Hall*	17 tons

Named for BM&L president. Built by Prescott, Scott & Company's Union Iron Works of San Francisco. Arrived Battle Mountain July 25, 1881. Placed in service August 12. Engine not accepted due to lack of power on 7% grade. Returned to builder and replacement ordered. Reportedly rebuilt as an 0-6-0T and possibly sold to R.D. Chandler & Co. (Chandler is known to have purchased PS&Co. 0-6-0T c/n 21-1881.)

| 2 | 0-6-0T | Union Iron | 27 | 1881 | *Starr Grove* | 14 x 16 cyl. |

Built by Prescott, Scott & Co. with 36" drivers. Named for major mine at Lewis. Original drawings show engine to be named *Star* (sic) *Grove*. Built as replacement for #1. Not delivered. Sold by PS&Co. to the Central American & Pacific Ry. & Transportation Co., Guatemala, S.A. (C.P. Huntington, Pres.) CA&P built Guatemala City-Esquintla (1884) and merged with Guatemala Central Ry. (1885). *Starr Grove* drawings made from original P.S.& Co. blueprints. Plans appear on page 63.

AUSTIN CITY RAILWAY 1880-1893

NO	TYPE	BUILDER	C/N	DATE	NAME	NOTES
1	0-4-2D	Baldwin	5586	1881	*Mules' Relief*	

A steam "Dummy" with enclosed body, 11 x 16 cylinders, 33" drivers. Wrecked morning of August 20, 1882 and rebuilt. Burned in enginehouse fire, February 1887. Moved to NC Shops for repairs in June 1893. Noted by NC as needing $150 in repairs, February 1898. Disposition uncertain. Donald Hofsommer reports sold to Acme Plaster Co., Quanah, TX (c. 1900). John Robinson reports this engine used by U.S. Reclamation Service on dam project in Southern Idaho (1911).

NEVADA CENTRAL MOTORS

Go Devil steam motor 0-4-0 built in Nevada Central shops (1882-3). Vertical boiler, 4-3/4"x 4-7/8" cylinders, 24" wheels, weight approx. 2,000 lbs. In "good order" (1898).

101 Fairbanks-Morse 2 cylinder, 4-wheel Shefield 1907 gasoline motor car.

102 Fairbanks-Morse 2 cylinder, 4-wheel Shefield 1909 gasoline motor car. Rebuilt with new body 1914. Wrecked December 1928.

103 Built by NC shops, with Fairbanks-Morse Shefield parts, 4-cylinder Ford motor 1914. Maroon body with green interior. Repowered with Model A Ford engine. (So hard to start they called it the "Bull of the Woods.") In use at end of operations (1938).

104 Vulcan Iron Works, 1917, 6-cylinder Wisconsin 100-h.p. gas engine. Ex-Argentine & Grays Peak #9. To NC 1920 and rebuilt with new body and rear baggage doors at a total cost of $6,300. Length 33', weight 10 tons. Built-in turntable. Out of service 1934.

105 A. Meister & Son, 1925, 4-cylinder Ford, 6 wheels. Length 23', width 7' and weighed 6,800 pounds. Traded to Eureka-Nevada Ry. for two side dump gondolas (1931). EN #23.

106 A. Meister & Son, 1926, 6-cylinder Buda gas, 8 wheels. Length 26' with built-in turntable. Set aside 1931.

107 Ford Model AA (1 1/2 ton) stake-body truck, 1928. Purchased from Nevada Central Motor Lines (1929) and rebuilt for rail use. In service at end of operations (1938).

Thanks to Gregory Maxwell for his research into the motor cars of the Nevada Central, much of which appeared in the Sagebrush Headlight, fall 1996 and winter 1997.

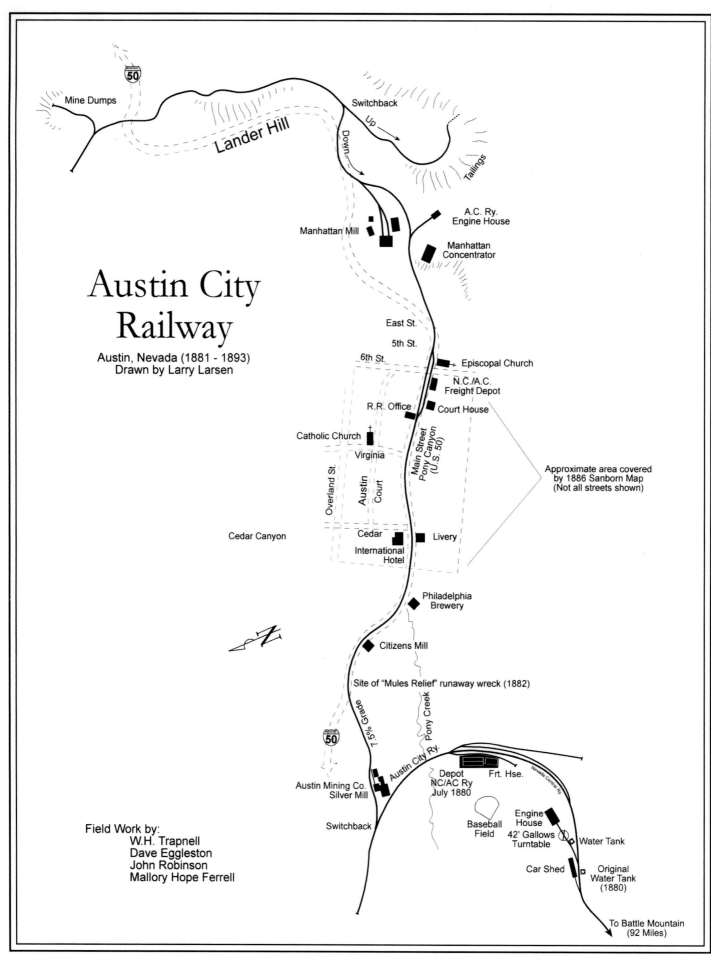

Mine Dumps

50

Switchback

Lander Hill

Up

Down

Tailings

A.C. Ry.
Engine House

Manhattan Mill

Manhattan
Concentrator

Austin City
Railway

Austin, Nevada (1881 - 1893)
Drawn by Larry Larsen

East St.

5th St.

6th St.

Episcopal Church

N.C./A.C.
Freight Depot

R.R. Office

Court House

Catholic Church

Virginia

Main Street
Pony Canyon
(U.S. 50)

Approximate area covered
by 1886 Sanborn Map
(Not all streets shown)

Cedar Canyon

Overland St.

Austin
Court

Cedar

International
Hotel

Livery

N

Philadelphia
Brewery

Citizens Mill

Site of "Mules Relief" runaway wreck (1882)

50

7.5% Grade

Austin City Ry.

Pony Creek

Nevada Central Ry.

Depot
NC/AC Ry
July 1880

Frt. Hse.

Austin Mining Co.
Silver Mill

Baseball
Field

Engine
House

42' Gallows
Turntable

Water Tank

Switchback

Field Work by:
  W.H. Trapnell
  Dave Eggleston
  John Robinson
  Mallory Hope Ferrell

Car Shed

Original
Water Tank
(1880)

To Battle Mountain
(92 Miles)

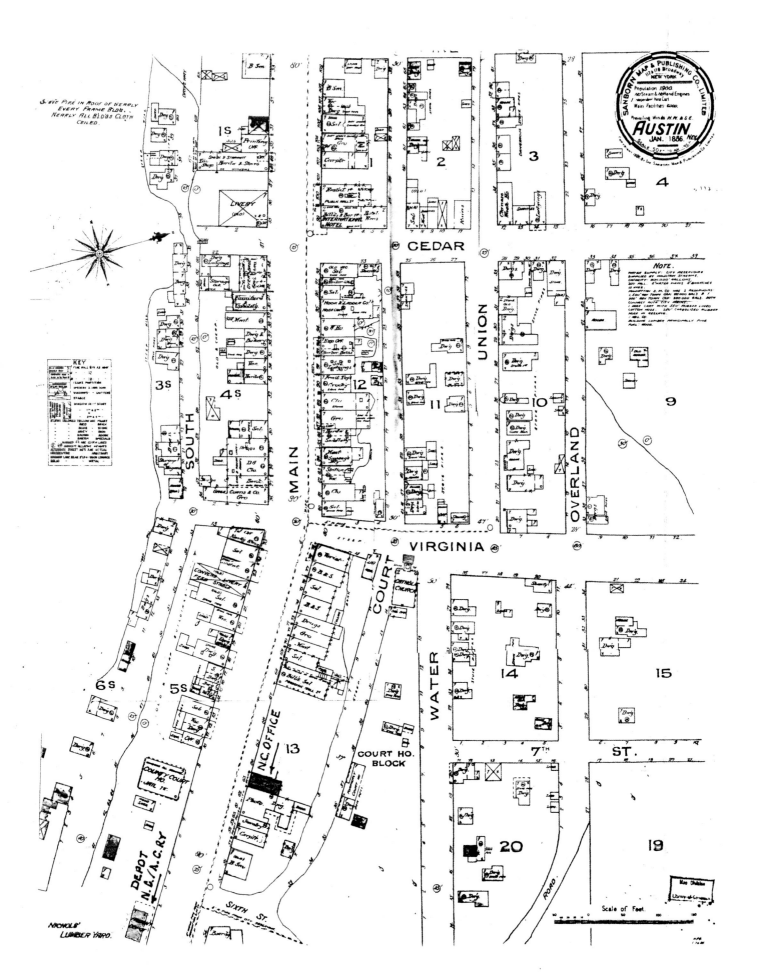

The tracks of the Austin City Railway ran up the middle of Austin's Main Street. The International Hotel and Catholic church are in the center, and mine dumps dot the distant hillside in this c.1890's view.
NENM

NEVADA CENTRAL PHOTOGRAPHS

Because of its remote locale in the virtually unpopulated cattle and sagebrush country of the Silver State, photographs of the Nevada Central, like its towns, are few and far between. This is especially apparent in the post-1900 period when the newness had worn off, and the glory days of the area's silver and gold mining ended.

The Great Depression years saw little railfan photography due to the NC's "off the beaten track" location and the expenses of travel and film. Photographic coverage of the road in the 1930s would be essentially non-existent had it not been for the efforts of the late Linwood Moody.

Railroad historian Moody was the Bellfast & Moosehead Lake RR agent in far off Union, Maine and was a noted authority on the Maine two-foot-gauge railroads. He began corresponding with an employee of the NC and sent him a postcard (3-A)-size camera and rolls of film.

Every few months Moody would receive and process the negatives, making contact prints for the employees, himself and trading prints with several friends like the late Gerald M. Best. Postcard size-prints for 10¢ each, plus 3¢ for postage, were offered.

Beginning in 1941, Linwood produced Moody's Magazine, which was devoted to obscure narrow gauge and short line railroads.

However, the publication was short-lived and becoming short of funds during WWII, Moody sold his negatives to Texas oilman Everett L. DeGolyer, Jr. Most of these are now in the DeGolyer Library at Southern Methodist University in Dallas.

CONTRIBUTORS

Gerald M. Best (d)
Edward Bond
Robert W. Brown
W. George Cook
Gordon S. Crowell
Robert Dockery (d)
Guy L. Dunscomb (d)
David Eggleston
Ted Gay
Grahame Hardy (d)
Paul Harr
Cornelius W. Hauck
Richard B. Jackson (d)
Fred Jukes (d)
Betty Kimball
Ward Kimball (d)
Gilbert Kneiss (d)
Pansilee Larson (NCNM)

Gregory Maxwell
Toni Mendive (NENM)
Arnold S. Menke
Herbert Merrill (d)
Jerry R. Mock
Otto C. Perry (d)
John E. Robinson
Frederic Shaw (d)
Richard F. Thomas (d)
Paul P. Thompson
H.W. Trapnell
Garrie L. Tufford
Harold K. Vollrath
Bert H. Ward (d)
T.L. Williamson (d)
C.W. Witbeck (d)
Ted G. Wurm (d)
Kyle K. Wyatt (CSRM)

ARTWORK/MAPS/PLANS
Robert D. Bailey
John Coker
Larry Larsen
Paul Nyeland (Courtesy Harold's Club, Reno, NV)
John Signor
Jim Scancarelli

ARCHIVES:
Austin City Museum
The Bancroft Library (University of California)
California State Railroad Museum (CSRM)
DeGolyer Library (Southern Methodist University)
Lincoln County Museum, Pioche, NV
Nevada Historical Society (NHS)
Nevada State Railroad Museum (NSRM)
North Central Nevada Museum (NCNM)
Northeastern Nevada Museum (NENM)
United States Geological Survey (USGS)
University of Nevada, Stokes Collection (UNR)

(d) indicates deceased at time of writing

BIBLIOGRAPHY

BOOKS

American Narrow Gauge Railroads, Hilton, George W., Stanford University Press, Stanford, CA 1990.

Austin, Past & Present, Banning, Jan, privately printed, Austin, NV 1977.

The Birth of California Narrow Gauge, MacGregor, Bruce, Stanford University Press, Stanford, CA 2003.

Bonanza Railroads, Kneiss, Gilbert H., Stanford University Press, Stanford, CA 1941.

Camels In Nevada, McDonald, Douglas, Nevada Publications, Las Vegas, NV 1986.

The Complete Nevada Traveler, Toll, David W., University of Nevada Press, Reno, NV 1976.

History of Nevada 1881, Thompson, Thomas H. & West, Albert A., Howell-North Books, Berkeley, CA (reproduction) 1958.

Nevada Central Valuation Report, Interstate Commerce Commission, Washington, D.C. 1917, revised 1927.

Mines of Battle Mountain, Reese River, et al, U.S. Geological Survey Bulletin 594, 1915 (reprint: Nevada Publications, Las Vegas, NV 1983).

Nevada Post Offices, Gamett, James & Paher, Stanley W., Nevada Publications, Las Vegas, NV 1983.

The Pony Express in Nevada, Mason, Dorothy, Nevada Bureau of Land Management, Harrah's Club, Reno, NV 1976.

Railroads of Nevada & Eastern California, Myrick, David F., Howell-North Books, Berkeley, CA, Vol. I 1962, Vol. II 1963.

Saddles & Spurs, Settle, Mary L. and Raymond W., Bonanza Books, New York, NY 1955.

Southern Pacific Narrow Gauge, Ferrell, Mallory Hope, PFM Books, Edmonds, WA 1982.

The Town That Died Laughing, Lewis, Oscar, University of Nevada Press, Reno, NV 1986.

Union Pacific Equipment 1885 Renumbering, Ehernberger, James L., published by the author, Cheyenne, WY 1989.

U.S. West, The Saga of Wells Fargo, Beebe, Lucius and Clegg, Charles M., E.P. Dutton, NY 1949.

Wells Fargo, Hungerford, Edward, Wells Fargo & Company, San Francisco, CA 1949.

Wells Fargo, Loomis, Noel M., Bramhall House, New York, NY 1958.

PERIODICALS & PAPERS

Battle Mountain Messenger, Battle Mountain, NV 1877-1882

Lander Free Press, Battle Mountain, NV 1881-1882

Central Nevadan, Battle Mountain, NV 1885-1907

Battle Mountain Herald, Battle Mountain, NV 1908-1910

Battle Mountain Scout, Battle Mountain, NV 1922, 1924, 1927

Reese River Reveille, Austin, NV 1880-1881-1901

Hammondsport Herald, Hammondsport, NY (various issues) 1879-1880

Humboldt Historian, Edaburn, Sharon L., "From Dream To Reality" Winter 1981

Baldwin Locomotive Works, specification books, drawings, extra order books, sales books, catalogs. DeGolyer Library, Southern Methodist University, Dallas, TX

Baldwin Locomotive Works, H.L. Broadbelt Collection Catalog, RR Museum of Pennsylvania, Strasburg, PA

Moody's Manual of Railroads, Moody Corporation, New York, NY 1900-1906 (various)

Narrow Gauge Equipment Studies, research staff, California State Railroad Museum, Sacramento, CA 1978-1979

Poor's Manual of Railroads, Poor, Henry V., H.V and H.W. Poor, New York, NY 1880-1928 (various)

Railroad Gazette, New York, NY 1880-1904 (various)

Railway Age, New York, NY April 30, 1885 (Go Devil)

This Was Nevada, Earl, Phillip I., Nevada Historical Society (A series of historical sketches appearing in many Nevada newspapers, 1991-1996.)

Western Railroader: CA & NV RR Historical Society, San Mateo, CA 1938-1988; 1988-2008 by Pacific Coast Chapter, R&LHS (various) "William Mason's Onward", Tufford, Garrie L. (Fall 1998) "Eureka & Palisade", Hauck, Cornelius W. (Fall 1997)

NEVADA CENTRAL AT A GLANCE

CORPORATE HISTORY

Nevada Central Railway Incorporated August 7, 1879
Acquired assets of Nevada Ry. (Incorporated April 1, 1878) on September 15, 1879
Road opened February 24, 1880
Acquired by Union Pacific Ry. June 16, 1881
Receiver appointed January 28, 1885 (after UP stock default)
Sold at foreclosure back to Stokes interests June 21, 1888
Reorganized as Nevada Central Railroad March 1, 1888
Abandonment approved by ICC December 20, 1937
Sold for scrap to Hyman-Michaels Co. January 31, 1938

Gauge: 36"
Miles of track (chained 1917): 92.178 (main), 3.229 (sidings)
Rail: 35# steel: 4 miles; 35# iron: 88 miles; 56# relay: 1 mile
Trestles: 66 (timber), total length 1,381

FACILITIES

Battle Mountain
Original Shop 20' x 50' frame 1880 (includes machine and blacksmith shops, supply room, locomotive shed)
Car Shop 20' x 86' frame 1880 (with connected sheds)
Carpenter Shop 20' x 40' frame 1887 (with two sheds)
Car Shed 16' x 116' frame 1887
Coal Bunker 104' x 17' 1897
Oil House 8' x 18' frame 1902 (with platform)
Paint Shop 1881
New Office 30' x 45' 1912 (two story)
New Shop Addition 60' x 60' corrugated iron on frame
Stock Yard 1887 on stub end of wye

CLIFTON (Austin)

Enginehouse 18' x 56' frame 1881
Car Shed c. 1902
Depot (1880) and freight house 16' x 88' (combined length)
Gallows turntable 42' c. 1881

WATER TANKS

Battle Mountain 14' dia. 10' high replaced 1880 tank in 1912
Dillon 8' dia. 7' 6" high 1910. Aermotor windmill 30' tower
Watts 13' 8" dia. 10' high 1907. Aermotor windmill 40' tower
Vaughn 13' 8" dia. 10' high 1914. Aermotor windmill 40' tower
Silver Creek 14' dia. 10' high 1907, carbody pumphouse 7'x 10' 1887
Ledlie 13' 8" dia. 10' high 1904. Aermotor windmill 40' tower, wye
Clifton: Original 1880 tank replaced by tank near enginehouse

Statistics from June 30, 1917. Inventory with additions.

Ward Kimball

203

INDEX

Compiled by Marilyn Heimburger